Social Leadership in Early Childhood Education and Care

Also Available from Bloomsbury

Peace Education, *edited by Monisha Bajaj and Maria Hantzopoulos*
Teacher Agency, *Mark Priestley, Gert Biesta and Sarah Robinson*
Successful Leadership in the Early Years, 2nd edition, *June O'Sullivan*
Educational Leadership for a More Sustainable World, *Mike Bottery*
Mentoring and Coaching in Early Childhood Education, *edited by Michael Gasper and Rosie Walker*
The Bloomsbury Handbook of Culture and Identity from Early Childhood to Early Adulthood, *edited by Ruth Wills, Marian de Souza, Jennifer Mata-McMahon, Mukhlis Abu Bakar and Cornelia Roux*

Social Leadership in Early Childhood Education and Care

An Introduction

June O'Sullivan and Mona Sakr

BLOOMSBURY ACADEMIC
LONDON • NEW YORK • OXFORD • NEW DELHI • SYDNEY

BLOOMSBURY ACADEMIC
Bloomsbury Publishing Plc
50 Bedford Square, London, WC1B 3DP, UK
1385 Broadway, New York, NY 10018, USA
29 Earlsfort Terrace, Dublin 2, Ireland

BLOOMSBURY, BLOOMSBURY ACADEMIC and the Diana logo are trademarks of
Bloomsbury Publishing Plc

First published in Great Britain 2022

Cover design: Charlotte James
Cover image © iStock / Getty Images Plus

Bloomsbury Publishing Plc does not have any control over, or responsibility for, any
third-party websites referred to or in this book. All internet addresses given in this
book were correct at the time of going to press. The author and publisher regret
any inconvenience caused if addresses have changed or sites have ceased
to exist, but can accept no responsibility for any such changes.

A catalogue record for this book is available from the British Library.

A catalog record for this book is available from the Library of Congress.

ISBN: HB: 978-1-3502-1215-2
         PB: 978-1-3502-1214-5
       ePDF: 978-1-3502-1216-9
      eBook: 978-1-3502-1217-6

Typeset by Integra Software Services Pvt. Ltd.
Printed and bound in Great Britain

To find out more about our authors and books visit www.bloomsbury.com
and sign up for our newsletters.

Contents

Figures

Acknowledgements

This book is based on a host of wonderful conversations with inspiring social leaders in ECEC around the world. We are deeply grateful to all of these leaders for their insights about social leadership, which were shared with such joy and generosity. Many other conversations have shaped this book and particularly those that happen in the context of our 'day jobs' at London Early Years Foundation and Middlesex University. We appreciate the many ways in which our colleagues put social leadership in ECEC into practice every day and continually share their learning. Finally, powerful conversations at home have had a role to play too of course. In this regard, June continues to be spurred on by the deep conversations provided by her colleagues, friends who are also social leaders, her husband Steve and son Fionn who constantly get her to think hard and deeply about leadership in education. Mona would like to thank her husband Tom for thought-provoking dialogues about what makes for transformational leadership in the context of an education system that needs to do better for so many children and young people.

Introduction

Welcome

In this book, we explore a new model of leadership in early childhood education and care (ECEC) called 'Social Leadership in Early Childhood Education and Care (SLECEC)'. In this introductory chapter, we aim to do four things. Firstly, we explain why we need a new model of ECEC leadership that puts social purpose at the centre of leading. Secondly, we define – in a nutshell – the model of social leadership. Thirdly, we tell the story of how the social leadership model came about and how it has developed over time. Finally, we provide an overview of the main chapters in this book, which are organized around the six elements of the SLECEC model.

Why do we need a new model of leadership in ECEC?

This book is based on the premise that we need a model of leadership that has at its core the commitment to leading with a social purpose. We talk about the protagonists of this model as 'social leaders'.

It is not particularly revolutionary to say that ECEC has a social purpose. Most of us who work in the field do so because we believe we can contribute to a better, fairer world. Research conducted by the Organisation for Economic Co-operation and Development (OECD) consistently shows that high quality ECEC can support children and families to thrive and is particularly important for those in contexts of poverty and disadvantage. In the UK, the Effective Preschool, Primary and Secondary Education (EPPSE) project (latest round of findings published in 2015) showed that high quality ECEC is associated with long-term academic outcomes and that this relationship is most robust for children with parents who have a lower level of educational qualification themselves. While ECEC's social purpose of supporting the learning and well-being of children and their families is generally recognized and embraced, the reality of the sector around the world is one of fragmentation and this is a barrier to effectively understanding and delivering the ECEC social purpose consistently and robustly across the globe.

This is certainly the case in the UK, the context closest to us as the authors of this book, but it is also commonplace in many other parts of the world. The fragmentation of the UK sector comes about as a result of government's lack of strategy and chronic under-investment, which results in a mixed economy of providers where the settings that serve those in disadvantage and poverty are most vulnerable. A lack of understanding among parents about just how important the early years are to a child's well-being and learning, as shown in the extensive research carried out by Ipsos Mori (2020) on behalf of the Royal Foundation of the Duke and Duchess of Cambridge, has enabled damaging ECEC policies to go unchecked for far too long.

ECEC in the UK is delivered through a high proportion of private provision, alongside charitable, social enterprise, community and state provision. Private providers have many business structures ranging from family-run single-site nurseries, childminders providing ECEC in their own homes right up to large nursery chains funded by private equity. While some of these businesses are able to generate large profits, contentiously channelled to shareholders, many are financially precarious and struggle to make ends meet year on year. In a recent Early Years Alliance (2020) survey, 25 per cent of private nurseries in the UK feared that they would not be able to survive the pandemic. Their unstable financial situation was a reality pre-Covid, which meant that many settings live 'hand to mouth'. The situation is not helped because such a mixed economy is challenging in terms of a shared voice, a clarity of social purpose and a collaborative approach. As a result different providers can see each other as competitors rather than partners in the aim of delivering the same social purpose.

The complexity, fragmentation and precariousness of the sector in the UK are echoed in many parts of the world. Grave policy challenges arise from funding mechanisms in ECEC that are far more diverse than is typically found for primary and secondary schooling. Globally, leaders of ECEC generally position themselves in a backdrop of mixed economy provision and in relation to multiple local and national government departments (Cheesman & Reed, 2019).

Another worldwide issue for ECEC is the composition and conditions of the workforce. A review produced by the OECD (2012), more than ten years ago, highlighted the wealth of evidence to show that 'high quality staff' in itself is not enough for high quality provision, since staff need to also be fairly treated and remunerated, and receive sufficient professional development. This triangle of support is more likely to drive high quality ECEC provision. The evidence for this has been further confirmed by the Education Policy Institute review (Bonetti, 2020). Many staff do not experience effective recruitment, high levels of retention and positive succession pathways though these are essential for developing the quality of ECEC, and in doing so, meeting the needs of children and families living in disadvantage. What we see is the opposite with many staff leaving the sector because they are dissatisfied by lack of status and value for their work, low pay and poor conditions and with no meaningful professional development opportunities.

Publicly and politically, the professionalism of those who work in ECEC is constantly under question and distorted by popular narratives that turn the noble work of ECEC into 'just childcare'. Two simple definitions describe ECEC. The first is an economic childcare service required by parents to enable them to work. The second is to support children from disadvantaged backgrounds to benefit educationally from the experience of ECEC. The second vision is less well articulated and the public do not fully understand the underpinning social purpose of ECEC which operates for both definitions (Ipsos Mori, 2020). We cannot even be sure that every government understands both of these purposes. In June 2021, as we write this introduction, Tulip Siddiq, Shadow Minister for Childcare and Early Education, asked in parliament about the concerning number of ECEC settings which had folded in the UK since the start of the year. She was told by the then Children's Minister, Vicky Ford, that what mattered was not whether numbers of settings were fluctuating but whether or not parents had sufficient childcare. Ford added that movement in the number of settings operating was normal because of 'mergers and acquisitions'. This response is questionable on many levels, but here we highlight the extent to which the current UK government openly prioritizes the quantity of 'childcare' places over the quality of ECEC provision. In doing so, they turn their back on the role that ECEC has been shown to play in increasing social mobility and reducing inequalities across a society. This is in the context of research showing that the educational attainment gap had already grown pre-pandemic (Hutchinson et al., 2019) and that children from lower socio-economic backgrounds have been more negatively affected by the pandemic (Education Endowment Foundation, 2021).

Children and families from backgrounds of disadvantage are often left behind unable to access or afford enough or the right kind of provision to support them to thrive socially and educationally (Early Years Alliance, 2020). In 2019, a UK Select Committee accused the UK ECEC system of 'entrenching disadvantage' because in reality, children from disadvantaged backgrounds spent less time in ECEC provision than children from more affluent contexts. This is a consequence of a fragmented mixed economy in which private providers struggle to make a profit because the funding available for the free at the point of delivery places to children from disadvantaged communities are significantly underfunded and providers are either unwilling or unable to subsidize the shortfall. In June 2021, The Early Years Alliance received the result of a Freedom of Information request to the UK Department of Education which proved that the Government knew that the cost of children would be £2billion by 2020, yet that invested only £300million.

So, while there is an assumption that ECEC has a social purpose the complex and messy realities on the ground mean that delivering this social purpose can feel an impossible task for many ECEC leaders.

We have written the book from the premise that the fragmentation of the sector has shaped how we consider ECEC leadership. Current models of ECEC leadership often share a narrative of a superhero leader overcoming the political, economic and professional challenges to run a well-oiled organization. Other models of leadership follow business leadership theories including defining leadership competencies with leaders learning how to balance the multiple needs of an organization including finances, people management, pedagogical leadership, community leadership, regulatory and inspection frameworks and so on. Douglass (2019) suggests for example that most literature on ECEC leadership thinks broadly in terms of two competing sets of functions for the

ECEC leader: pedagogical leadership and administration. She highlights the sense in the literature that there is always too much for the ECEC leader to balance explaining that 'studies have examined the challenges ECEC leaders face, such as tensions around the broad scope of their role and competing demands on their time' (p. 13).

O'Sullivan (2015) designed a model, shown above, to explore all the elements of leadership necessary to drive an effective ECEC social enterprise which continues to surprise new staff as to the many layers of leaders under the simple term of ECEC leader.

In their review of the literature on leadership in ECEC over the last twenty years, Nicholson et al. (2020) conclude that:

> *A large percentage of literature does not include explicit discussion of social justice in theorizing about leadership. A growing number of studies discuss equity issues within the body of the manuscript including the gendered nature of the field or low compensation rates. However, there is a lack of connection between these inequities and the definitions or purposes of leadership for the field.*

As a result, the under-investment in the sector and the poor policy decisions from the top have robbed the sector not only of its capacity to enact a social purpose, but even of its readiness to lead with social purpose at the fore. We need therefore decisively and explicitly to bring social purpose back to the heart of how we think and talk about leadership in ECEC.

Rethinking leadership and leadership development is an important process to meet the contextual issues of the time. Facing up to modern challenges nudges us into reconsidering if the existing leadership models work to deliver a social purpose. Getting leadership and leadership development in ECEC right is 'crucial for enabling learning, pedagogy, participation, distributed power, voice, challenge, stimulation, social equity, democracy, community and achievement to flourish in a positive and purposeful climate' (Cheesman & Reed, 2019, p. 183). The stakes are high.

We are not arguing that ECEC currently has no one leading with a social purpose. There is an important difference between saying that there is a gap in terms of how we model leadership as opposed to the actual reality. We advocate that by modelling and narrating the leadership of those who already lead with a social purpose in ECEC we can encourage more conversations about social leadership. Modelling social leadership is helpful because it supports and inspires readers to understand their own leadership. It also furthers our understanding of the conditions that support SLECEC to flourish and we can then agitate and advocate for these conditions more effectively.

A note on context

The difficult context outlined above is not applicable in every single part of the world. Some societies have established ECEC policies, in which the sector – including for the very youngest children – is an established and sustainable part of the education system. We are thinking here for example of the world-famous ECEC systems operating in Scandinavian countries. Sadly, this is not the case in the UK or in many other countries which are still trying to ensure that ECEC is embedded and well understood in national policy. The SLECEC model is designed with these difficult contexts in mind. While we hope it will still be useful to those in parts of the world where ECEC is better provided for, our understanding of what constitutes 'social purpose' is not only about improving lives across society and reducing inequalities, but also about securing a sustainable future for ECEC and its workforce.

What is social leadership?

In a nutshell, social leaders in ECEC lead with a social purpose to create an organizational culture and pedagogical approach that fosters a fairer society for children and families, framed within economic, social and environmental sustainability and impact.

To deepen our understanding, we can consider each part of this definition in turn.

Social leaders

We describe 'social leaders' as those who lead with a social purpose. It is an important part of this model that social leadership is not exclusive to those occupying formal leadership and management positions within ECEC organizations. The model is relevant to anyone working within ECEC, whether they are an apprentice or a manager. However, we have written this book primarily for leaders who are shaping their organizations to develop a culture for social leadership. While this is our main focus, Chapter 4 explores how and why social leaders need to build a culture that will invest in the leadership of others on the understanding that everyone can be a leader as part of their everyday professionalism.

Early Childhood Education and Care (ECEC)

Throughout the book, we refer to 'early childhood education and care' (ECEC). We use this term for two reasons. Firstly, it captures the breadth of what we are trying to do in this sector, which is a combination of education and care for the youngest children. In other books (Sakr & O'Sullivan, 2021), we have used the term 'early childhood education' (ECE) on the basis that education includes a dimension of care anyway and therefore this does not need to be stipulated separately through the addition of 'and care'. However, we are happy to be more explicit in adopting the phrase 'and care' to make it clear that working with the youngest children and their families is about learning and caring and that neither of these elements can or should be removed from the mix. Secondly, the term is internationally recognized. For example, it is the term preferred in the reports produced by the Organisation for Economic Co-operation and Development (OECD). It therefore helps to position social leadership as a global model, which is very much in line with the intentions of this book.

Organizational culture

Given the current fragmentation of the ECEC sector in many parts of the world, and the contribution of policy-makers to this fragmentation, we place great importance on the work of organizations within ECEC. Organizations may be providers of any kind and size. It is through organizations – at least to begin with – that social leaders can have a significant impact on the ground and their contributions can shape the nature of ECEC. Our understanding of culture is a collection of learned values, behaviours, attitudes and practices shared by the organization.

All of the elements in the social leadership model relate to organizational culture, but there is a particular focus on its power in the following elements:

- Creating a culture of collaborative innovation
- Investing in others' leadership
- Facilitating powerful conversations

Pedagogical approach

A social pedagogy is key to the model of social leadership. It is central to social leadership as in too many parts of the sector, pedagogy continues to be the 'silent partner' (Stephen, 2010). If ECEC is to be an effective vehicle for social change we argue that we need to understand how to shape a social pedagogy to fulfil the social purpose of ECEC.

Social purpose

When we talk about 'social purpose', we are referring to the work people do in order to create a better, fairer society. Some refer to this as 'social justice' including Nicholson et al. (2020) in their important review of the literature on ECEC leadership. While we have used this term elsewhere, we have decided not to use it when shaping our definition of social leadership. Instead, we chose to reflect the words and phrases most often used by the social leaders we interviewed. They tended to talk in terms of 'social purpose', creating an inclusive space for conversations about purpose, vision and leadership. In this space, leaders used the terms that made the most sense to them and better supported their leadership stories of social purpose in action.

Economic, social and environmental sustainability and impact

Social enterprises are businesses that operate a triple bottom line: delivering economic, social and environmental impact. While we are clear that social leadership is not exclusive to social enterprise organizations, we consider this kind of organizational framework to be highly conducive to social leadership. In some of the conversations we had writing this book, leaders would say 'I think I lead a social enterprise but I just haven't realised it before'. What is expressed through this statement is that there is a space for hybridity within ECEC that many social leaders occupy. Our exploration of ECEC social leadership highlighted how social enterprise can flourish in this hybrid space. Other academics have argued vociferously that the solution to the current fragmentation of ECEC is universal state provision that extends from birth to five. While we respect this view, our vision of what is needed is different and we place more faith in what can be achieved through social enterprise or 'doing business by doing good'. So as part of understanding what social leadership is, we adopted the triple bottom line definition.

How did the model come about?

In the early summer of 2019, Mona wrote an email to June asking to spend some time in London Early Years Foundation (LEYF) to explore how leadership was designed, implemented and understood on the ground in the context of a social enterprise ECEC provider. June agreed because as someone who had already written about leading a social enterprise she was interested in having the model examined by someone outside of the organization, especially as the organization had doubled in size using the leadership model and she was keen to evaluate progress, identify areas for improvement and consider if the models of embedding change were working.

Later that summer, Mona spent time in four LEYF settings, each with its own story in the social enterprise context. One of the settings served a fairly affluent community and made a profit (known internally as 'financial impact') to support colleagues in a sister nursery that was loss-leading but delivered high levels of social impact through extensive cross subsidization of government funded places. The remaining two nurseries had a more mixed intake and essentially 'broke even'. Across these four settings, Mona carried out eighteen interviews about the nature of leadership within LEYF. These interviews ranged from conversations with apprentices who had only recently joined the organization and were not sure about their future in ECEC, to managers with more than twenty-five years of experience in LEYF.

Mona was amazed at the way in which individuals across the organization, even those who had only recently joined and were relatively new to the sector, could talk about leadership so openly. Until this experience, she had never realized just how reluctantly her own university students, on an Early Childhood Studies undergraduate degree, talked about themselves as leaders. This prompted her to see leadership in ECEC quite differently – as an organizational dimension that could help to transform the sector and something that had been denied to the sector through the marginalization of those who work in it.

Discussing the findings of these interviews with June and Lorenzo Chiozzi (Head of People and Performance at LEYF) prompted new questions about the nature of social leadership in ECEC. We reflected together on the use of the term 'social leadership' in business (e.g. Guglielmo & Palsule, 2014) and the extent of its relevance to thinking about ECEC. In business, social leadership is about developing innovation, agility and responsiveness in organizational culture by drawing on the talents and ideas of everyone in the organization. It involves avoiding traditional hierarchies and creating a culture, as well as systems and processes, that support leaders to harness 'social energy' across the organization. While this seemed to resonate with some of what had emerged in the LEYF interviews (e.g. avoiding hierarchical behaviours), we talked about the need to make our social purpose more explicit. This would mean that a model of social leadership in ECEC would not just be about how things were done, but why they were done.

We realized that to move our thinking on, we needed to hear from other ECEC leaders around the world who we suspected were social leaders. We needed to hear from them about what they thought this model might be, how it might work and whether what we'd found in the context of LEYF would resonate for them too.

Together, we carried out fifteen interviews with leaders in ECEC around the world. To recruit leaders to participate in these in-depth dialogues, we described our idea for social leadership and if people felt affinity with the bones of that idea, they came on board to discuss it further.

These dialogues have been fulfilling and thrilling experiences. The richness and thoughtfulness of those dialogues are the reason why this book exists and we cannot express our gratitude enough to those below:

- Jacqueline Lamb, CEO of Indigo Childcare Group, Glasgow, Scotland
- Julian Grenier, Head Teacher of Sheringham Nursery School, London, England
- Chantal Williams, CEO of Stepping Stones Children's Services, Tasmania, Australia
- Peter Frampton (Executive Director), Nicola Maguire (Director of Early Years), Dan Wise (Senior Director, Children and Families) and Katrina Estey (Director of School Age), Learning Enrichment Foundation, Toronto, Canada
- Alice Sharp, CEO of Experiential Play, Glasgow, Scotland
- Nichole Leigh Mosty, former director of Ösp Playschool, Reykjavik, Iceland
- Dearbhala Cox-Giffin, Director of Childcare at Giraffe Childcare, Dublin, Ireland
- Zaridah (Zee) Abu Zarin, CEO and founder of Horizon Centre of Excellence, Kuala Lumpur, Malaysia
- Brett Wigdortz, CEO of Tiney, London, England
- Professor Nurper Ulkuer, Child Development Expert, UNICEF, Ankara, Turkey
- Ed Vainker, CEO of the Reach Foundation, London, England
- Barbra Blender and Eliana Elias, ECEC Coaches, California, US
- Cassie Holland, Manager of Archfield House Nursery and co-founder of the Bristol Beach Schools, Bristol, England
- Mandy Cuttler, Head of Pedagogy, London Early Years Foundation (LEYF) and Nick Corlett, Senior Nursery Manager and Sustainability Lead at LEYF
- Pauline Walmsley, CEO of Early Years – the organization for young children, Belfast, Northern Ireland

You can see from the list that there is some diversity in terms of national context, with colleagues contributing from Australia, Canada, Iceland, Ireland, England, Malaysia, Scotland, Turkey and the United States but of course there are so many contexts that we have not brought into the discussions *yet*. These conversations offer a rich starting point for developing a model of social leadership in ECEC, but at this point we offer the model as a work in progress. Ideally, we will deepen our work with more conversations, dialogues, workshops and open forum discussions cutting across diverse contexts around the world. Another important kind of diversity it is worth highlighting is the organizational contexts of leaders. Contributors come from the context of private, state, charitable and social enterprise provision. Social leadership in ECEC was not ruled out by any one of these contexts and that is exciting because it suggests a means of leading that cuts through the various models with a social purpose focus.

Dialogues began with an assertion that ECEC has a social purpose, and then a discussion about what this means for leadership. Lasting 90 minutes, each discussion was rich with stories and perspectives and philosophical stances that had often been developed over a lifetime of work in the sector. We carried out an iterative thematic analysis on the transcripts of the interviews, working through rounds of analysis until we arrived at a model – the model presented in this book – that felt right.

When we talk about what 'felt right', we are talking about praxis. Praxis, as explained by Paolo Freire in Pedagogy of the Oppressed, is the coming together of reflection and action, in order to critically reflect on social realities and then seek to transform them. Analysis and model-building happened in a space that brought together June's career, the practice of LEYF, the perspectives of the social leaders we spoke to and the reflective work of coding and thematic organization.

Social leadership in ECEC: the model

The model is made up of six elements, shown below. These are aspects of leadership that social leaders put their energy into and which make significant change. In this sense, they are 'drivers' or 'levers' – they are the points at which social leaders apply pressure in order to create the maximum impact.

Who this book is for?

This book is for leaders and aspiring leaders in ECEC. While readers will bring different perspectives and levels of experience to discussions of leadership in ECEC and to making sense of SLECEC, we are writing for those willing to re-design their organizational culture and re-think their pedagogical approach in ECEC contexts. Regardless of your official role or title, whether a new or experienced leader in any type of setting, we hope that the act of reading the book can infuse your daily conversations with personal and professional examples of what happens in your setting and how this connects you and your colleagues in deeper professional conversations about social purpose.

We want you to critically engage by bringing your own practice and experience to bear. Question and challenge what we tell you on the basis of what you see around you. Even better, bring the issues to the staff meeting for further discussion and reflection. Create a reading group with colleagues or fellow students where you can use what we share to provoke further debate about the social leadership model and where you and your colleagues see yourselves in relation to social leadership. Be brave, have conversations and see where they lead.

Overview of the book

We have organized the book so that each main chapter is an exploration of one of the six elements of social leadership in ECEC. In each of these chapters, we consider three questions – why, what and how. This means that we consider (1) why we need that particular element in social leadership, (2) what the element looks and feels like on the ground and (3) how it is generated, developed or supported in context through social leadership. To answer these questions, we draw on existing literature but also on the practices of LEYF as our main case study weaving throughout the book as well as the reflections and examples from our fifteen interviews with social leaders around the world. We also draw on written contributions kindly offered by Anne Patterson and Keya Lamba, comments made by Professor Julie Nicholson in the context of an Early Years Leadership Symposium hosted by BELMAS (co-convened by Mona and Dr Maddy Findon) and a wide range of conversations that are part of our day-to-day work and research. It would be impossible to name all those who have influenced the development of the social leadership approach, but we hope that they will accept our general expression of gratitude and acknowledgement. Below, we briefly outline each of the six elements and the corresponding chapters.

Leading with social purpose

Social leadership starts and ends with social purpose. There is no social leadership without social purpose. This means that social leaders must have a clear vision of how ECEC contributes to a better, fairer society. In this chapter, we probe the interactions between ECEC and social purpose, investigate diverse manifestations of social purpose and explore what it means – in practice – to drive ECEC forward through a commitment to social purpose.

Implementing a social pedagogy

Social leaders understand that ECEC pedagogies are the way through which social purpose can be realized. If social purpose is the heart of social leadership, social pedagogy is the heartbeat – it is the process through which the social purpose does its work and brings life to the organization. In this chapter, we consider the evidence to demonstrate that pedagogies and pedagogical leadership are an essential part of achieving an ECEC that really can contribute to a fairer society.

We outline the dimensions of a social pedagogy – that is, a pedagogy through which a social purpose can be achieved, and we explore how social leaders enact social pedagogies through their everyday work.

Creating a culture of collaborative innovation

Social leaders are committed to radical levels of collaboration, often upsetting the status quo in order to bring about the partnerships that they know will make a fundamental difference to the children and families they serve, as well as the professionals that are the backbone of ECEC. In this chapter, we consider what a culture of collaborative innovation looks and feels like, and through examples, we explore the difference that it can make to the work of organizations and their capacity to achieve their intended social purpose.

Investing in others' leadership

Social leaders are quick to give their power away, investing a lot of time and energy in developing the leadership of others. They commit to a language of leadership as part of the organizational culture, thinking and talking about leadership openly and inclusively so that it feels like a part of every professional's working life and approach. They do this to enhance sustainability across the sector, recognizing that there is a severe shortage of leadership across ECEC and a worrying lack of systematic leadership development. In this chapter, we explore why leadership development is so essential to the future of ECEC and its social purpose, as well as how social leaders demonstrate their commitment to the leadership capacities of all professionals in the sector.

Facilitating powerful conversations

Powerful conversations are needed in order to achieve all the other elements in this model of leadership. A powerful conversation is one that leads to change – it might change someone's mind about something, it might change intended and subsequent actions, it might change how someone reflects on something that has happened already or what they want for the future. Powerful conversations can be pedagogical conversations (to implement a social pedagogy successfully), coaching conversations (to grow the leadership of others), reflective professional conversations (to embed a culture of collaborative innovation) and wider network and public conversations (to grow the sense of social purpose in ECEC, and within this, sowing the seeds of sustainability across the sector). In this chapter, we look at each of these types of conversation in more detail but also consider general principles that sit across different types of conversation – the principles that unleash the power of powerful conversations: trust, empathy, risk-taking and challenge.

Sowing the seeds of sustainability

Sustainability is finally moving to the centre of the political and public agenda. This is good news as we face huge global issues including poverty, lack of education, climate change, environmental degradation, water scarcity, biodiversity loss, pollution, food insecurity and food waste and disease. This may seem completely disconnected from the world of ECEC but a central tenet of our work is to prepare children to undertake their roles and responsibilities as accountable global citizens. The seventeen UN Sustainable Development Goals include SDG number 4 which requires us to ensure inclusive and equitable quality education and the promotion of lifelong learning opportunities for all. Education is a powerful pathway to sustainability, but it depends on adults who understand how to integrate sustainability into every element of their leadership, pedagogy and operational practice. Solutions for a sustainable, flourishing world requires a new model of leadership that can foster a sustainability mindset, that places economic, social and environmental sustainability at the heart of the service and ensures we pass a flourishing world that is better than the one we inherited to a future generation.

Final note

We hope that you enjoy reading this book. We believe in the power of conversations and we hope that the book feels more like a conversation than a traditional academic text. It is an invitation to think with us about social leadership in ECEC and its future. We present a working model rather than a finished product, and the development of the model belongs to all of us. Where we take this depends on our dialogues, reflection and actions. Please share your thoughts with us. Tweet your ideas, intentions and actions as you read the book and afterwards. Together we can deepen and embed this new way of leading.

June @JuneOSullivan
Mona @DrMonaSakr

1

Committing to a social purpose

In this chapter, we explore how and why social leaders need to commit to a social purpose in ECEC. We ask:

- What do we understand by social purpose in ECEC?
- Why must social leaders promote the importance of social purpose in ECEC?
- How can social leaders drive social purpose in ECEC?

What do we understand by social purpose in ECEC?

When organizations and businesses describe their social purpose, they refer to the reason for their existence: the ways they want to create a better world or be an engine for good and a positive force in society. Organizations that drive a social purpose can be formed in many ways.

LEYF is a social enterprise and is constituted within a charitable governance structure so that it can blend together social and commercial goals in the pursuit of a fairer society by designing social enterprise nurseries where over one-third of the places are subsidized to enable children from poor and disadvantaged communities to access high-quality ECEC operating a social pedagogy (see Chapter 2). Indigo Childcare Group in Scotland and Learning Enrichment Foundation in Canada use a similar model to deliver their social purpose while Early Years in Northern Ireland is a more traditional charity with heavier reliance on grants and fundraising.

Stepping Stones in Australia, Experiential Play in Scotland and Horizon Centre of Early Childhood in Malaysia are commercial businesses, but still have a strong social purpose running right through their constitution and their activities. State provision of ECEC, which may be in the form of playschools (the

Scandinavian model), maintained nursery schools (as in the UK) or nurseries that sit within schools (as with the nursery at Reach Academy in London) are all founded on a strong social purpose.

While social leadership in ECEC must involve a strong sense of social purpose, there is flexibility as to how ECEC professionals within organizations connect with this purpose and how exactly they define the purpose. Some focus exclusively on the child's experience and their learning, while others focus more on what is happening around the child, such as the family, the staff and the wider community. The common element is that they want to create a more equitable world and do this by enabling all children, and particularly those experiencing disadvantage, to access high-quality ECEC provision that is supportive, ambitious and accessible. Jacqueline Lamb describes the approach at Indigo Childcare Group:

> *I think as far as our governance terms are concerned, they've always been about supporting families in areas of deprivation to get back into work. That's the technical aspect of the governance. In my view, it's a lot bigger than that. I think there are two strands to it. It's about breaking that generational cycle of poverty, because it's so deeply entrenched here in Castlemilk (an area of Glasgow, Scotland). And alongside that, it's about doing something to close that attainment gap – whatever contribution you can make to close that attainment gap, to contribute to breaking that cycle of poverty … It's about inspiring new families that comes through to reach for the best that they can possibly reach for regardless of where they're coming from and the experiences they've had.*

How we articulate social purpose will depend on the specific context in which we work. For Pauline Walmsey, leading the charity Early Years in Northern Ireland, the social purpose is about supporting children and families to thrive in the context of a peaceful society:

> *From the beginning, 55 years ago when our organisation was developed it began from a child-centred perspective. Our vision was and remains 'children are strong, confident and visible in their own community', 'children are emotionally and physically well', 'children are respectful of difference' and 'children grow up in a peaceful and shared society'. This is something very important for us in Northern Ireland. Our social purpose is to promote and develop high quality evidence-informed early childhood services for young children and their families. That has remained the purpose of the organisation going back to when those founding mothers met in 1965. That's why they came together, to try and develop and further their practice with the children they were working with at the time, and we have continued to place that purpose very centrally in the organisation.*

For Alice Sharp, leading what she describes as a private limited Early Years Training Company in Scotland, there is a similar focus on supporting local communities through ECEC:

> *My company came from me buying the Scottish Independent Nurseries Association and reshaping it so I could run courses that reflected the challenges we were facing such as teaching staff how to walk with fragile families and gathering expertise from organisations such as Sheffield Children's Centre and LEYF – I wanted to be much more focused on a social purpose of equity and access and that kind of clashed with the Board, which were not about that, so very quickly they offered me the opportunity to buy the company. As a teacher I'd never wanted to own a company. I hate being responsible for staff salaries. It's the bit of the job I worry about the most. It's never been on my radar. But what I've loved is the change of ethos that my ownership gives me, I can now choose the purpose that we have, and although we're a limited company, at the heart of what we do is how we can help change communities. Making profit out of that sits uncomfortably with me but we have to pay staff salaries and we have to invest in the future. You're always fighting against the attitude of 'oh that's a limited company, we're not giving them any money' but what they fail to understand is that we're investing it back, so I believe we are socially motivated, even though it might not say it explicitly in our paperwork.*

This stance also resonates with Chantal Williams from Stepping Stones in Australia, who focuses more closely on the needs of parents – often single mothers living in relatively isolated areas – and how parents can be supported through ECEC:

> *Well, the very first Centre we set up was because people didn't have access to childcare. The centre that was already in our town was catering just for people who were working and they didn't have any spare places. In Australia you have to run by the guidelines which is that people working or studying have to come first, children at risk of some sort of abuse have to come second, and then it pretty much all falls away for everyone else. We wanted to change that and open up spaces for everybody else. And some of my favourite memories over the last 25 years have been parents coming in, more often than not, single mums, and they'd come up to the counter and wouldn't even look you in the eye, they would be looking down and have their child with them and say 'I just want to see if he can come here, maybe just once a week' and we'd say 'yes have you made your list?' and they'd say 'what list?' and we'd say 'of all the things you can do when you're on your own'. 'Ahhh no no, it's not about me'. And I'd say 'yes it is about you – it's as much about you as it is about your child'. And they'd start to stand up a bit straighter because someone heard them and someone could see that they needed some time. They just needed*

a hot cup of coffee that they could drink to the end, to visit a friend or do the shopping or the housework without the children running around behind them. So, for us it was about providing care to empower – to give parents time to ease their load, to have someone else to talk to. Sometimes they didn't have anyone else. And we would be it. So, whilst we do have lots of and lots of working parents, we are quite often that person who will listen. But their children have a chance to get out and about and meet other children as well. So for us, it's a no-brainer that if you're working you need childcare. But we really promote the social aspect of childcare and for us giving parents a break is as much important ass giving their children an opportunity to learn and develop in childcare.

It can be confusing for social leaders to make sense of the social purpose that drives them, particularly when they are operating in the context of private business. When we wrote to Zaridah Abu Zarin in Malaysia, owner and manager of the Horizon Early Childhood Centre in Kuala Lumpur, she commented:

To be honest with you June, I have never thought of myself as a social leader but more of a business owner. In Malaysia the term social business is only recently introduced. All I know is that I am paying my staff much higher than the rate most practitioners are getting paid and trying my best to share good practices that I carry from the time I worked at LEYF.

Many of us think about national systems of compulsory education as a basic 'social right', designed to equalize people's life chances by compensating for social disadvantage (Gilbert, 2010). We talk about schools as giving everyone the skills to get a job and participate fully in society. However, Gilbert suggests that this vision has essentially failed and while schools can make a difference to people's life chances, in general they do not, and, in many cases, they actively reproduce social inequities, a point also made forcefully by Fullan and Quinn (2016).

In terms of social purpose, the ECEC sector paints an even more complicated picture than other parts of the education system because many of the ECEC models are shaped by market forces. According to the OECD (2019) most countries continue to have low-funded ECEC services despite the UNCRC recognizing that child's right to free and accessible ECEC. In the UK, the ECEC sector grew as a response to Tony Blair's announcement when he became prime minister that poverty was solved by employment and therefore a childcare infrastructure was necessary. This led to the first National Childcare Strategy in 1998, when money was set aside to build nurseries and children's centres and respond to the real paucity of available childcare. Twenty years on and the landscape has changed. Subsequent governments have added to childcare provision through occasional financial and policy incentives, but it has been haphazard and driven by short-term initiatives and projects. Consequently, social leaders have been uncomfortable with leaving the response to poverty and disadvantage entirely to the market because there is no history of the market fully addressing inequality of education provision especially when funding is inadequate. Most subsidies are given directly to parents through the funded entitlement, the universal credit childcare element, working tax credits and tax-free childcare. According to the National Audit Office (2020) parents find there is an insufficiency of ECEC places in disadvantaged areas particularly for flexible childcare, childcare for atypical hours, or places for children with SEND. Private providers complain that operating in such neighbourhoods is not financially viable.

Understanding social purpose in ECEC depends on understanding the national policy context. Childcare in the UK, where we write from, provides a £6.7billion annual contribution to the national economy and is a key part of our social infrastructure. There are over 24,000 nurseries with 1.1 million places for children. According to the independent UK-based ECEC research body Ceeda (2019), private, voluntary and independent nurseries are responsible for 80 per cent of childcare places in England and employ over 250,000 staff in a workforce of 365,000. Most English nurseries (71 per cent) are defined as 'Mommas and Poppas' which describes the one or two nurseries with a single owner. Next in line are the groups of three and four nurseries which constitute 10 per cent, then we have the groups of five to nineteen nurseries which also constitute 10 per cent of the sector and the biggest groups of twenty plus nurseries are 9 per cent of the market. Together all the nurseries offer 1,064,677 places. Childminder numbers are falling but there are still 37,299 providing 240,724 places. However, once you look deeper less than 20 per cent of those settings are focused on providing children from disadvantage with a significant number of places and the continual reason is that they cannot afford to subsidize the Government contribution towards funding 'free' places for children whose families cannot afford the full cost of nursery.

Across the world we are seeing movement in the ECEC market space driven by the increased involvement of international venture capitalists in the sector. These are groups of investors who form a partnership to provide capital to businesses which seem to have high growth potential in exchange for an equity stake. The Venture Capital fund will invest and nurture the growth of those businesses with a view to sell with a substantial return on the investment.

There is also a new route to investment in the sector from social investors. Like venture capitalists, they raise money but choose to invest in companies that are actively creating positive social or environmental change by consciously tackling society's challenges. Of course, they also want to make some form of financial return. Much of the funding from social investors is debt at a high interest rate to cover their set up and management costs.

There are concerns about the rise of the venture capitalist involvement in the sector. The language of investors talking about lively market opportunities and overseas investment portfolios can be uncomfortable and for many completely at odds with the conversation of social purpose, pedagogy and quality. Scandals like Southern Cross in the social care sector and the ABC Nursery chain in Australia caused consternation. Southern Cross private equity funded care homes over-extended themselves and ran out of cash, causing the business to collapse. The Australian ABC nursery chain, which had become the biggest in the world, went into liquidation in 2008 as a result of burdening itself with debt while chasing aggressive expansion. It was simply too big to fail and the Australian Government had to provide a bailout of millions to keep the nurseries running until new buyers took over. Interestingly, the biggest provider to rescue ABC was the social enterprise partnership Goodstart.

A report from NEF (2019) argues that services run increasingly by globalized chains focus on provision of large settings in high-end areas with decline in places in more disadvantaged areas and a 48 per cent rise in affluent areas. The consequence can be 'childcare deserts', which are geographical areas without sufficient childcare. These are more likely to fall in areas where ECEC would serve low-income communities, rural communities, families of colour and families with irregular working patterns (Zeng et al., 2021). Reich (2019) notes a corresponding increase in hyper competitiveness among parents especially in the United States as they worry about getting their children into the best preschool to increase their chances of becoming successful and getting into the best school so parents can feel confident that they are passing their economic status to their children and in doing so creating even more rigid class divisions. Marianne Cooper (2020) tracked the increasing unequal income distribution and the corresponding financial and emotional burden on families where parents' anxiety about financial security has led to a frenzy of intensive parenting. The economists Doepke and Zilibotti (2019) explain that in countries with high social inequality, such as the United States and China, parents are required to do far more to support and prepare their children, because business and government do so little. This reality stands in contrast to low-social-inequality countries with more family-friendly policies.

Given this complex global context, the debate about social purpose in ECEC is timely as we negotiate the best systems to build more equity for the youngest children and their families. Social purpose as a common good resonates from all the social leaders we interviewed. For social leaders, it is about providing a means of making ECEC accessible to children from disadvantaged and poor backgrounds while ensuring all efforts to embed continuous improvement to drive quality. Operationally, this can be achieved in different ways, whether through a strong social business and pedagogy model at LEYF or higher remuneration for staff provided by Zaridah Abu Zarin or Alice Sharp developing training and support for poor families to help them leverage better educational and financial outcomes for them and their families.

Why must social leaders promote the importance of social purpose in ECEC?

Social leaders actively seek out disadvantage and look for ways to respond. Many social leaders are also social entrepreneurs and that is unsurprising. Social entrepreneurs seek out complex issues and try and create a business or organizational response to address the issue but in a way that empowers those experiencing the problems. They also generally reject the deficit narrative associated with disadvantage and reframe it both positively and creatively. Social leaders accept that while building an organization is desirable, the main purpose for social leadership is to lead with a purpose and shape a service that encourages a balanced focus on economic profits, employee well-being and social and ecological impact.

One of the biggest challenges to social leaders in ECEC is how to address child poverty, a situation which produces social and economic inequity with manifold negative outcomes for everyone. Left unaddressed, poverty can alter the trajectory of a child's entire life increasing the likelihood of long-term poverty, poor educational outcomes, developing obesity, mental health issues as well as dying early. Poverty is the strongest statistical predictor of how well a child will achieve at school. At the end of primary school, pupils living in poverty are often over nine months behind their peers in reading, writing and maths. For example, in the UK, the Child Poverty Action Group (CPAG) report (2020) states that children with a high persistence of poverty (those on free school meals for over 80 per cent of their time at school) have a learning gap of 22.7 months – twice that of children with a low persistence of poverty (those on free schools' meals for less than 20 per cent of their time at school), who have a learning gap of 11.3 months.

The attainment gap persists for pupils throughout secondary school. UK Students eligible for free school meals are half as likely to achieve a good pass at GCSE in English and Maths in comparison to other students living in poverty who are four times more likely to be permanently excluded from school than their peers. And finally, even when disadvantaged students gain the same qualifications as their peers, they are 50 per cent more likely to be Not in Education, Employment, or Training (NEET). Sadly, this pattern is also evident in other rich Western economies (Fullan & Quinn, 2016).

Even though the UK is the fifth richest economy in the world, poverty exists in every corner of the UK. To be defined as living in poverty, families live in a household with less than 60 per cent of the national median income. A total of 14.5 million people are living in poverty and of those, 4.2 million are children, with those under the age of five the hardest hit. This means that when we look at a class of thirty children in a classroom, nine of those children are living in poverty and the number is likely to get even higher due to the impact of the Covid-pandemic. The Legatum Institute Report (2020) suggested that due to the pandemic, a further 690,000 people have been pushed into poverty, of whom 120,000 are children. For these families, the crisis has multiplied their struggle to balance insecure work, low pay and a patchy welfare system while trying to cover the cost of essentials like soaring rents, food, fuel bills, transport and childcare. Poverty rarely has a single cause. It is created by a range of factors including rising living and housing costs, low pay, insecure work or lack of sufficient working hours, and inadequate social security benefits. Mohammed Yunus (2007) points out that poverty is not created by poor people but by the systems we have built, the institutions we have designed and the concepts we have formulated.

Access to high-quality affordable childcare in local communities is accepted as central to supporting the reduction of some elements of child poverty and social leaders in ECEC identify this inequality and commit to making a measurable positive impact for disadvantaged children. However, if ECEC is one way of responding to poverty, then it needs to be underpinned by solid, consistent policy support and funding so it is possible to deliver the highest quality provision for all children. Currently, this is not the case in many parts of the world. For example, in the UK families with two parents working full-time earning the national minimum wage are still 11 per cent short of the income needed to raise a child to reach their sixteenth birthday.

The concerns about how ECEC is funded in the UK become even clearer when you read a report published on 15 June 2021 following a Freedom of Information request by the Early Learning Alliance, that stated in 2015 the Government had predicted that the cost of ECEC in the UK would be £2billion but in reality they provided just £300million which meant the hourly subsidy provided to settings to support children's education was short by nearly £3 an hour. This is a policy that means ECEC providers continually remain underfunded and have to be willing to pick up the shortfall themselves or risk going under. Those settings in areas of poverty and deprivation are more likely to be negatively affected, and thus so are the children and families they would serve. ECEC providers in disadvantaged areas are more susceptible to financial difficulties, because of fewer parents using childcare and face challenges in terms of remaining sustainable and improving quality (Ofsted Annual Report, 2011; National Audit Office, 2020).

There is no ECEC without staff, yet their status is low and unrecognized and their access to training is underfunded and inconsistent. This is despite a strong thread of research, from The Effective Preschool, Primary and Secondary Education (EPPSE) Study (Department for Education, 2015), showing that well-trained staff make the most impact for children's learning. Staff need to be properly rewarded and remunerated, yet the model we persist in pushing counters this because underfunding means it is difficult to make ends meet and if most of the service is made up of small family run business. Without proper funding it is very difficult to build a financial margin into their business models to provide higher salaries. In the UK, the requirement to pay the national living wage is welcome but it increased over the past three years by 16

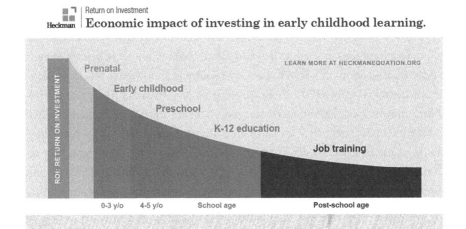

Figure 1.1 Heckman Curve.

per cent while the government funding rates increased by less than 2 per cent. For organizations like LEYF operating in London trying to achieve the London Living Wage while operating within the same funding gap among populations with higher levels of disadvantage, requires financial wizardry. According to the Christie & Co. annual report 2019, the UK has the lowest investment in ECEC compared with France, Germany and Scandinavia. This seems short-sighted in light of Professor James Heckman's Curve which illustrates the highest economic and social returns come from earliest investment in children (see figure 1.1).

The Covid pandemic has impacted negatively on the sustainability of an already precarious sector. The NDNA (2020) survey showed that 71 per cent providers in England expect to operate at a loss with a further 23 per cent breaking even. The Coram Annual Childcare survey (2021) and the Department for Education's own research recognized the impact of Covid on a sector where, pre-pandemic, many nurseries were already operating at a loss or only just breaking even as a result of chronic underfunding. The Greater London Authority Report in March 2021 found that childcare providers across London are struggling to survive due to the challenges from the pandemic which caused significant increases in overheads as well as substantial reductions in income. Unsurprisingly, those in deprived areas were hardest hit with a staggering 70 per cent of nurseries in disadvantaged areas 'struggling' compared with 59 per cent in more affluent areas.

This is the tip of the iceberg when it comes to the issues that social leaders face in leading with a social purpose. Another major battleground are the attitudes and discourses that surround ECEC, children and families. For example, Donald Simpson (2019) found staff working in areas of deprivation thought poverty was a problem of troubled parenting. Few attributed it to factors such as low pay and unemployment. The researchers analysed 179 questionnaires and 30 interviews across four countries and found that respondents held relatively negative views about children in poverty relative to their better off peers. This negative attitude affected the ECEC professionals' views of children's cognitive ability, motor skills, emotional development, health, respectfulness and ability to stay on task. There was also evidence that they did not adjust how they taught or made any amendments for those children, yet a sizeable minority of children enter settings with needs related to their disadvantage. They sought support from the depleted Local Authority support teams only when a child had an identified developmental delay.

The views among staff about parents living in poverty were equally negative particularly about issues such as attendance at meetings, volunteering at the setting, responses to communication and engagement in their children's learning. Such unconscious and conscious attitudes may be undermining and fatalistic for those children attending and deepen the disadvantage for those very children who can least afford it.

In this deeply complex context – which we have only really touched upon – social leaders take on the structural issues of child poverty despite the hostile policy environment and the challenges of attitude and understanding. Social leaders will find ways to reduce or remove the constraints that poverty places on people by deepening the conversations and demonstrating why and how ECEC can be transformational.

How can social leaders ensure social purpose is strengthened by their leadership?

Leadership is an ever-evolving concept. What we think a leader does and is depends on our context. The research story of leadership and the resulting raft of more than 1000 studies all concluded that leadership is not a simple concept and none of these studies have produced a clear profile of the ideal leader. Given that leadership cannot be separated from the societal context in which we operate, it is unlikely that there is one model of ideal leadership. We understand leadership as a process that allows someone to lead change in individuals, organizations and across the sector. If we want to focus leadership in ECEC on achieving a social purpose, it can be helpful to think about previous iterations of leadership in ECEC and how views of leadership in the sector have changed over time. From this foundation, we can start to develop the concept of leadership further so that it helps us to lead with social purpose.

During the 1990s, theories of leadership began to enter into discussions of ECEC in a concerted way. Models that had developed in other sectors were transported across, and modified in order to suit the needs of leaders working in ECEC. Jillian Rodd (1996) was one of the first researchers to identify leadership characteristics from the business world that would be helpful to those leading in ECEC, so that they could more effectively respond to the policy changes that were driving a fast-changing sector. This started a trend demonstrated in 2004 with the development of the National Standards for School Leadership or the work of Bottery (2004) who argued for six professional requirements to guide educational leaders to frame their understanding and actions not only within the organization but in managing its boundaries and in responding to and participating in future proposals for professional formation. Three years later, Aubrey et al. (2013) produced further work on ECEC leadership competency in line with wider business thinking and the popular approach that leaders needed to have a set of competencies to lead their organization. The result was ten years of organizations of all sizes and structures developing a set of competencies to frame their leadership expectation. They generally focused on planning and organizing, professional expertise, interpersonal skills and working in partnership.

More nuanced research, specifically focusing on ECEC leadership has shown us that there is no such thing as a list of ideal characteristics and competencies of an ECEC leader (Nicholson and Maniates, 2016; Douglass, 2017; Nicholson et al., 2020). These studies show that leadership cannot be divorced from the social context in which we operate. Having said this though, there remain processes that are important and helpful to leadership in ECEC. For example, Nicholson and Maniates (2016) highlight the importance of reflection and reflexivity in the development of the ECEC leader and Douglass (2017) highlights the importance of an entrepreneurial approach (what she calls 'leadership from within') to responsively address the many and changing challenges of the sector. What leadership processes come to the fore when we look at the work of delivering on a social purpose? In our dialogues with global leaders in ECEC, we asked them what helped them to keep social purpose at the centre of their leadership. Five strong messages emerged:

1. Build the vision and share the story
2. Agitate, innovate and embrace change
3. Build an empathetic values-driven culture
4. Create a pragmatic social purpose operating environment
5. Become a learning social leader

Build the vision and share the story

The first message we heard from leaders was the importance of identifying the social purpose. People need to know what they are signing up to and they want to hear this from the social leader. Everyone needs to know clearly and unambiguously what role they play in delivering the social purpose. Social leaders are good storytellers and they can bring alive everyone's role in delivering the social purpose.

Zaridah Abu Zarin, CEO of the Horizon Early Childhood Centre in Kuala Lumpur, talked together with her sister Zarita about the importance of sharing the story of early childhood and the role it plays in a person's learning and well-being throughout their life. They wanted to change the attitudes of not just professionals in the centre, but also parents and family members, so that they would understand the importance of early childhood experiences and focus on making these the best possible experiences they could be. To make the message come alive, Zee and her sisters shared the story of their own early years, when their parents tragically died. Telling the story of what they went through and how they developed resilience which has been with them ever since helped to bring both ECEC professionals and parents on board with the understanding that what experiences we support children to have will have an impact on who they become.

Social leaders begin by setting out the vision and the strategic steps that will be used to achieve the social purpose. They tell the story in a way that amplifies the role everyone plays in achieving the purpose whether you are in the support service such as the Finance Officer, the Customer Service Executive or the Marketing Assistant or the nursery teacher. Using storytelling to set out the vision is not to be underestimated and it also offers staff a form of social proof because they are influenced by what they hear and like being part of the group.

Many organizations try and simplify the essence of the story with a slogan. For example, the LEYF slogan is 'Changing the world one child at a time' so staff understand that every engagement with a child helps to achieve the social purpose which is to provide the highest quality ECEC for all children but especially those who come from disadvantaged backgrounds.

Social leaders need to understand how to tell the story not in the traditional, hierarchal over-curated way but in a way that like a case study gives examples and illustrates the varying roles of everyone in the story. Our social purpose is often emotive and therefore we need to be sensitive to the different audiences and how they receive the story so they want to work with us to meet the social purpose. For example, the LEYF model is based on a fee structure where the profit from fair fees to more affluent families is used to subsidize affordable and accessible places for children from poorer communities and disadvantaged backgrounds. Some families paying full fees may not be convinced by this model, therefore how we tell the story of how their contribution adds to the social purpose must be convincing and transparent. Social leaders need to make quite deliberate efforts to share the story of the social purpose and to remember to share it not just with staff but to parents and wider stakeholders.

Agitate, innovate and embrace change

Social leaders who have their social purpose right at the heart of their leadership are attuned and responsive to the continual changes which could impact on that purpose. In social purpose organizations, we are often asked about our theory of change. In other words how our resources are transformed through our activities and their results into the achievements we were hoping to deliver. For example, LEYF has developed a model of high-quality ECEC for children from disadvantaged backgrounds. We therefore need to be clear how all our resources including our social pedagogy, staff training and qualifications, nutritious food from the Early Years Chef Academy and the fees we collect are used to create the high-quality nurseries we need to lead, develop and integrate across London ensuring we continue to subsidize at least one-third of the places. Once social leaders are clear about their theory of change, they also need to be responsive to both internal changes which drive improvement and external contextual changes and be able to integrate both kinds of change vertically and horizontally at every level of their organizations.

Ed Vainker from Reach Academy was thoughtful in how he thinks we can navigate change and talks about his partnerships in West London.

> *I'm inspired by the Harlem children's zone, but the criticism of the hub up to now has been programmes before people, and we're now launching a collective impact project based on a model from the States called Strive Together, and so that's something that we're building. We've also done quite a lot of work with Citizens UK to build a community organizing network in Feltham. It's deliberately designed to be a collective impact approach. We're focusing on leadership across the board. It's half institutions, half members of the community. We're starting with education providers, so we've got early years, schools and a university. We're trying to take a different approach – it's deliberately very iterative, generative, we're very lucky that we've got funding for it for seven years which is exciting because we can build it and take the necessary time.*

Driving social purpose takes a lot of energy and many social leaders are part of a social movement which can in itself strengthen the social purpose. For example, LEYF has been at the vanguard of the social enterprise movement for many years. Social leaders will stand up publicly for what they believe to be right. They don't just espouse empty platitudes but are brave and willing to learn, empower and fight for equality, for fairness, for what is right, whatever the cost. Social leaders will engage in movements which rise out of frustration with educational policy which they perceive fails to consider how children learn or rail against the lack of progress on reducing child poverty. Reflect on the caustic comments of Sir Al Aynsley-Green in his 2018 book about the betrayal of childhood for children in Britain. He refers to the response from the Minister of Childcare at the time who ignored an attempt to explore the concerns of many in the sector about the suitability of the curriculum:

> *it's hardly surprising that there is so much unhappiness among teachers in England when genuine attempts to get dialogue was so appallingly brushed aside with such stunning arrogance.*

(p. 38)

Nowadays, movements emerge through social media where the conversation spills into action and social leaders are right in the middle of the action. Peter Drucker, the well-known management writer, argued that future problems are rooted in outdated assumptions about how things ought to work. These problems are solved when leaders and followers begin to think differently together. Ultimately, successful social movements persuade people to act in support of a shared common cause that needs to be part of a future change even though the immediate steps are difficult.

Social leaders need to be agile and flexible in their responses to change and understand the power of pivoting. This was never more obvious than during Covid, when many ECEC organizations pivoted at speed to deliver new services to meet unexpected need. For example, many ECEC organizations delivered digital home learning services, created food banks and delivered food parcels, toy packs, fundraised for additional places for children in need as well as improved internal systems. A common mantra of many social leaders is to never waste a good crisis.

Peter Frampton at Learning Enrichment Foundation in Ontario highlighted the need for responsiveness in leadership underpinned by a social purpose:

> *There's no shortage of poverty and there's no shortage of great ideas. So if you, and the staff are going through life with their minds and arms open and putting effort into how to say yes, then there's no end with what you can be engaged in. and as long as the leadership exists to push it, then it has a bit of independence and it can flow. Sometimes it's not just the right moment for things and you allow them to go into furlough and their day will come another day. So that kind of openness,*

approaching the world from a lens of not scarcity, but a lens of actually incredible
richness allows for an awful lot to happen.

When trying to find solutions to intractable issues such as child poverty
or sustainability, we reflect on a statement attributed to Nelson Mandela
reminding leaders that they must do many things at once to adapt and execute
simultaneously; similar to crossing and building the bridge at the same time!
This is echoed in a comment from Alice Sharp, CEO of Experiential Play in
Glasgow, Scotland, who explains that:

as a leader you have to be a bit different, pushing at the boundaries, always
questioning 'is that really what we want to do? Is that enough?'

Social leaders need to understand how to bring about change. A model of change
favoured by LEYF is called the ADKAR model developed by Jeff Hiatt in 2003
and introduced as a practical tool by Prosci, a renowned change management
consultancy and learning centre. The ADKAR (Awareness, Desire, Knowledge,
Ability and Reinforcement) model is mainly intended to be a coaching and
change management tool to help and assist employees through the change
process within organizations. The name ADKAR stands for a sequential set
of activities that shape how staff will respond to change, as well as providing a
simple format that includes the means of embedding the change so it works. The
intention is to help tell the story of change but also help social leaders stop and
reflect at each stage and critically review progress in partnership with staff and
in a way that is built into the system. At LEYF, this is particularly important as we
integrate settings into the organization which have been stand-alone community
nurseries trying to deliver a social purpose but unable to remain financially
sustainable. Many nurseries arrive in an unplanned way and we therefore need
to understand that change is continual and central to our social purpose to help
ECEC settings in disadvantaged areas, which are constantly at risk of failing
from fast changing social circumstances and policy decisions.

Fullan and Quinn (2016) talk about the importance of using relevant data
that provides evidence to make changes for the better. Using an example of work
done in schools in Canada where students were continually failing, they provided
examples of where schools improved using push-pull strategies. For example, he
described the pull strategy as accessing the data which could eliminate excuses
that students' lack of progress was based on their background and circumstance
and the push strategy was to create three teams in the school to focus on how
and what changes needed to be made to data collection and the necessary
curriculum and teaching which could improve the school at every level. Each

team involved the head teacher and invited teachers to join. The outcome of the involvement was solid and embedded improvement.

Once positive change gets moving, the challenge is how to sustain it because driving social purpose means that the cycle will never be finished and we have to look at ways to scale our social impact. To address this, social leaders need to foster an ethos of innovation by attracting and selecting talented staff, providing a culture of trust and exploration, synthesizing the learning gleaned from the innovation, providing communications pathways vertically and horizontally in the organization and celebrating each step of the evolving change. No one says it is easy! The tensions in managing all of these parts of the process are highlighted by Barbra Blender and Eliana Elias, ECEC coaches from First Five in San Francisco:

> *we can empower from the ground up and we can make differences from the ground up, but to make true lasting change, it has to be a systemic overhaul.*

Build an empathetic values-driven culture

The power of empathetic relationships and the importance of a shared culture which is values-driven builds trust and is underpinned by kindness and empathy was mentioned over and over in our dialogues. Social leaders saw that the social purpose would be more successfully delivered when the whole organization was working together.

According to many of the social leaders we interviewed the importance of kindness in leadership and the language of kindness is particularly relevant to the ECEC sector but also an antidote for the unkindness that can be fuelled by an uncontrolled social media. The word 'kind' is important in ECEC as it is linked to the German word for children 'kinder' and therefore resonant with how we in ECEC nurture and nourish children. Rousseau thought children were instinctively kind, and that humans respond to others in need. At LEYF, children learn that being kind to others provides them with a protective cloak which means others are more likely to be kind back.

Baker and O' Malley (2008) list the six ingredients of kindness including compassion, gratitude, authenticity, integrity, humility and humour. Humour is often not recognized for its potential to create a warm atmosphere in which people listen empathetically and connect with each other which can lead to a virtuous cycle of collaboration and willingness to be kind to each other.

According to Garnett (2018), empathy and kindness are crucial for our mental health because they allow us to create bonds of trust that give insights into what others are feeling or thinking and therefore help us to better understand how and why people respond to situations. A leader who recognizes this is likely to build an organization where people work together and understand each other and that will lead to impressive organizational results because:

> 'empathy reduces prejudice and fights inequality and creates peace. Research also demonstrates that empathy deepens intimacy, boost relationships reduces bullying promotes heroic acts and even succeeds where brutality fails.'

> (Garnett, 2018, p. 26)

In ECEC, empathy is often aligned to acts of kindness, but in reality kindness is most meaningful when it is a way of being rather than a set of random acts. Doing one act of kindness does not cut the mustard nor does confusing kindness with being nice. According to Prasad (2008), kindness can be learnt, nurtured and developed so it becomes central to how you live your life. Of course, the cynics in us recognize those who use kindness for their egotistical benefits such as getting on or playing the social status game.

Kindness needs to become part of the values of the organization. When it is integral to an organization, it ensures that kind leaders are aware of their broader impact not just the impact on business results. People are central to the success of the organization by sharing their ideas, problem-solving and delivering over and above. They need to be treated accordingly, including valuing a diversity of views, ideas and opinions. Haskins et al. (2018) found that kindness had an ameliorative effect on personal anxieties, increased empathy and built personal trust and psychological stability.

> The acts of kindness in leadership manifest in multiple ways, namely, respecting, caring and responsiveness, a personal touch and a humane approach. The leaders respond with acts of kindness towards people when they face personal problems. These acts may be directed at three levels – community, organisation, teams and individuals.

> ((Johri)Haskins et al., 2018, p. 81)

Some people in business associate being kind with being weak but, kindness requires mental toughness. This means keeping calm and positive while holding the social purpose right at the heart of the issue that is being negotiated. For example, during Covid, the importance of accessing funding for places for children from disadvantaged backgrounds required a balance of kind negotiation underpinned by a mental toughness to steer the campaign so that we would get the funding. Philips and Taylor (2009) explain that although there has been a shift in business practices to more competitive individualism and independence in order to make a bigger profit, this approach has also been criticized as leaving no place for the kind-hearted. The Harvard Business School research report in January 2017 found that having a kind leader creates improved interpersonal relationships, drives others to do good deeds and reinforces other kind behaviours. According to Leadbeater (2020, p. 10):

> *too much kindness without any challenge is naïve; too much challenge without any kindness can be harsh. But when kindness and challenge are combined it can be transformational.*

Mark Carney, ex Head of the Bank of England (2020), has recently written about the importance of values and how we need a new social contract founded on fairness, personal responsibility, sustainability and solidarity. The kind leader creates an organization that will treat staff fairly. The reward is measurable in loyalty and trust which results in positive engagement, reduced staff turnover, and staff who are aligned to their organizations' values and willing to accept decisions that are sometimes uncomfortable. For example, during Covid, several organizations made changes to HR policies such as holiday pay which temporarily reduced staff's terms and conditions to a minimum statutory level but did so with the full support of their staff. Zaridah Abu Zarin from Horizon Centre of Early Childhood in Malaysia reflected on her response during Covid.

> *this was the time when I needed to make sure that my staff are well looked after. I decided to close the centre because I thought if Covid is in the building, we need to cool down for about two weeks, and then we can start operating again. That's how I saw it. Also, for me to be able to sustain during this time, we had to be creative and think about how the Horizon Centre was going to survive, so we sent the teachers out to students' homes, and gave them loans to start their own businesses online – it might be a little amount of money, but as a leader, I have make sure that my staff are well looked after. That's the soft side of me.*

Leaders who are honest, open and transparent enjoy the trust of their employees. Many of these characteristics point to a high level of emotional intelligence, which can lead to better management and better retention of staff. This is important in ECEC where staff turnover is a significant problem. A study from Norwich University Online Leadership Programme found that employees who had managers with high emotional intelligence were four times less likely to leave their company and that more than 70 per cent of their perception of the company culture resulted from these manager's emotional intelligence levels. Focusing on the work and the people while also learning to listen and respond empathically are two ways not only to become a better leader, but to boost the productivity of the team. Ed Vaniker reflects on the way that this has worked at the Reach Academy, and as part of the wider work of the Reach Foundation:

> *Our work comes from a huge commitment to children fundamentally. I think that's what it's all about really. And because we work really hard to build those strong relationships with parents, from empathy and a feeling of shared responsibility with the parents for what happens to that child.*

By engaging them in big strategy decisions, understanding their perspectives and then acting on them, staff feel valued and engaged which reinforces their loyalty and trust. Recently, this was tested by the Covid pandemic. Leaders who had embedded trust could engage staff fully in solving the complicated problems which emerged from navigating a pandemic. For example, social leaders in ECEC were able to respond with agility to the situation – delivering essential services to keyworkers while keeping the children safe. At the same time, they embraced digital technology to keep staff trained and engaged and create home learning digital platforms and apps at speed to keep the children and their parents connected.

Being a social leader is more than just knowing there is a team, it is knowing how to cultivate trust, care and respect within the team. These values within the team will allow all the members to share ideas and collaborate, creating a more open atmosphere from which everyone has more of stake in leading the company through an ever-changing economic climate. Accomplishing extraordinary things in organizations is hard work. To keep hope and determination alive social leaders must recognize each contribution and tell the story so everyone can see how the action, decision or change strengthens the social purpose of the organization.

A noble social purpose needs a pragmatic operating environment

The social leaders we interviewed talked about credibility and integrity and being able to walk the walk and talk the talk. They described doing this by building what we call a flexible pragmatic operating system aligned to the organizational values, with inbuilt systems, processes and practices that allow agile and flexible responses to ensure we continually deliver our social purpose.

Social leaders develop an operations system that drives the social purpose. According to Harvard Business School, the pioneering studies of service industries in the early 2000s found that a primary driver of satisfaction among employees is the knowledge that their company is delivering results to happy customers.

Translating this into an ECEC context, LEYF operates a social purpose operating environment aiming to connect the parents and staff with the systems, so they understand and value what is done behind the scenes. This builds stronger relationships as it is clearer to parents how the behind the scenes work is driven by social purpose and in turn drives social purpose. It also supports parents to understand the expertise of the professionals, to appreciate the effort and quality of what goes on and the value they place on the service increases. The same for staff, who became much more engaged when they understand the impact of what they do on children, parents and colleagues in the organization. For example at LEYF finance and customer services staff are based in nurseries regularly so they can see how their systems can either make things easier or more complicated for nursery staff and parents. This led to a review of the systems including seeking the opinions of staff and parents through surveys and focus groups so we could make them more streamlined and logical and more clearly aligned to our social purpose. Dig deeper in ECEC and we need to understand this thinking with regards to the child, the parent, the staff member, the contractor and any other stakeholder. Do we design the welcome pack to meet the needs of all our parents? Is the signage on the nursery welcoming in the neighbourhood? Are the systems for registering the child accessible and easy to operate? Do we create recruitment advertising that welcomes staff from the local communities? During Covid, the role of the ECEC teacher became much clearer to many parents as we delivered a digital home learning experience. So many more parents began to realize just how much we do to provide an integrated care and education to their children.

This approach is important in social purpose organizations, where sometimes services designed to work with children and families living in poverty or disadvantage lack ambition, are cumbersome and bureaucratic and the service is at best mediocre led by indifferent, or powerless staff. We do not always have the best website or high-end technology partly because it takes longer to fund the support services. The importance of a strong infrastructure is often mis-understood in a social purpose organization. But investment in the infrastructure services such as customer services, administration and communication, fee support is essential (Zeng et al., 2021). For many parents who live on tight incomes, understanding how to access available hours, knowing when they need to pay fees, understanding financial support such as food is essential before they can even consider the pedagogical benefits for their children. This is just as important for employees also. Our support services such as the HR function, the availability of training and development and the ease by which staff can get relevant information about their salaries, hours or concerns is important. It is the first step towards social purpose in any organization and social leaders need to be alert to every level of service delivery across the organization. Too often we focus all our attention on the frontline delivery but fail to invest in high-quality support services at our peril. Every effort must be made to employ the capable and engaged staff to deliver the highest quality support services if we are to achieve our social purpose.

Social leaders need to create operational transparent processes, including technology so the processes are more visible, can improve experiences and allow for regular critical reviews and a feedback loop that fosters in employees a greater sense of purpose, helps families accessing the service feel better cared for and ultimately improves trust in the organization which strengthens long-term relationships.

Become a *learning* social leader

If social leaders are to ensure the social purpose weaves through the organizational culture and underpins the strategic and operational activities and targets, then it is helpful if the social leader is also a learning leader. This means being alert to what is happening inside and outside the organization. A learning leader will want to know how we learn as an organization from the top-down to the bottom-up and everything in between. Learning leaders need to ask questions constantly about the organizational approach to learning and if we can innovate in response to the challenges we face. A learning leader wants to test ideas and reflect on what is happening within the organization such as the impact of changes to systems, or the learning from the induction of new staff.

Social leaders understand the importance of communication and reflection as well as the need to build a collaborative culture where there is a focus on performance which is assessed and monitored. Leaders seek to influence rather than command change. As a result, they show humility, are always prepared to listen, are highly approachable and like to get 'stuck in' alongside the team. Leaders use information from their walking the walk to identify what is going well and what needs to be reviewed and improved. For example, are staff supported to extend their learning in a way which both strengthens their own leadership but moves the organization towards achieving the vision? Have we built in an approach to action research which supports staff learning and development? As Pascal and Bertram (2012) note, we miss great opportunities by not developing a culture of professional enquiry. Shared dialogue is one effective means of developing a culture of enquiry and social leaders need to be good conversationalists and good listeners if they are to learn what is happening across the organization. The enquiry is about understanding the broader issues across the organization as opposed to professional enquiry that drives independent development. That also needs to be part of the operational processes.

Social leaders create an environment which encourages conversations and builds harmonious relationships in which people are ready to listen and work with each other. The process of a conversation is complex and therefore provides an opportunity to address different levels of information, learning and exchange. The focus lies upon coming to some greater understanding rather than winning the argument.

Social leaders also need to root out where things need improvement if they are to really make a difference. There is no point imagining that everything is rose-tinted as that leads to mediocrity and sometimes poor practice. Social leaders need to be courageous and willing to face those problems head on and you will only do that if you are visible and constantly asking questions, observing, reflecting and building a culture of openness and dialogue. Pauline Walmsley from Early Education in Northern Ireland is refreshingly honest here.

> It's all about advocating for an investment in quality provision for young children … demonstrating what the impacts and the outcome of that quality is in terms of the life of the child and family and community and the government, those are the strategies and the techniques that you need to use. It is also about prompting a little fear by demonstrating that poor quality practice can be really harmful and how it can harm children, and then building understanding then about how you put in place that quality, and the impact that that can have on society.

Conclusion

In this chapter, we have explored the role of social purpose in how we design our ECEC organizations and deliver our service to sustain an equilibrium between the economic, social, ethical, educational and environmental ecosystems so as to benefit the whole of society.

Social leaders passionately believe that they can make a difference and are able to persuade others to see how each person can contribute to delivering social purpose for the future. We noted that it was important to find ways to ensure staff fully understood their role in delivering that social purpose and how all decisions would be taken to strengthen and add value to the social purpose.

We asked why social leaders needed to demonstrate the importance of social purpose and why social leaders must give everyone in their organization from the child to the staff member a voice so they can facilitate conversations that challenge, inform, question and extend learning about ECEC. The role of the social leader is to create a culture of continuous improvement with a focus on refining and improving pedagogy so that it deepens children's learning. Social leaders initiate conversations at every level. They form a community of learners and together reimagine how services and support for children and their families are delivered. They co-create meaning with children, families and professionals in ECEC rather than accepting the status quo without question. Social leading is a mindset to rebel, to reach out and seek expertise and be unafraid to ask 'why?'.

Finally, we explored how social leaders promote the importance of social purpose in ECEC. We identified that this was very much through the culture that shaped the organization, the key activities of the social leader and the means by which they acted so that staff trusted them and followed them. Being kind, compassionate and empathetic is essential in order to shape a culture of mutual respect, reflection and teamwork underpinned by transparent operations to sustain the extraordinary efforts of all the staff who want to deliver their social purpose. Social leaders need to stand up and agitate for what they believe will support their social purpose but do it in a way that is thoughtful and reflective so when things change or don't work be able and willing to acknowledge, rethink and make the changes. Social leaders need to be constantly learning about their subject and invite other views and opinions to enrich the learning so the service is always in touch with those for whom it is designed.

Social Leadership in ECEC is hands-on, non-hierarchical, warm and inclusive. These characteristics resonate with those found more generally in the literature on Social Leadership. According to research across all manner of organizations, Social Leaders seek to influence rather than command change. As a result, they show humility, are always prepared to listen, are highly approachable and like to get 'stuck in' alongside the team. As Julian Stodd (2014, p. 16) advises:

> *We are in the social age of learning. Formal hierarchies count for less than our social communities and ability to create meaning.*

2

Driving a social pedagogy

This chapter explores social pedagogy as a means through which social leaders deliver their social purpose. We consider the evidence to demonstrate that a social pedagogy and pedagogical leadership are an essential part of achieving an ECEC that can contribute to a fairer society. We outline the dimensions of a social pedagogy – that is, a pedagogy through which a social purpose can be achieved, and we explore how social leaders enact social pedagogies through their everyday work. We address three key questions:

1. What is social pedagogy?
2. Why should social leaders support social pedagogy?
3. How does social pedagogy strengthen social leadership?

What is social pedagogy?

Social pedagogy has a long history which evolved from the thinking of Greek philosophers Plato and Aristotle who understood that education goes way beyond educational institutions and brings together ethical, political and pedagogical issues in a way that is significant to society as a whole. The term 'social pedagogy' was first used by German educationalist Karl Mager in 1844. He created an educational solution to social and economic upheaval which challenged social integration by blending the theory of social and moral education into a method of practice. The result was a set of ideas based on the values of humanity. These ideas were never static but continually reviewed and refreshed by thinkers and practitioners who refine their pedagogical responses to changing political, social and economic issues with the ultimate intention to create a more just society through educational means. Consequently, social pedagogy has developed in somewhat different ways across different countries over time, and has been deepened by great pioneering theorists of education such as Johann Amos Comenius, Johann Heinrich Pestalozzi and John Dewey and more modern thinkers such as Bronfenbrenner, Freire and in the pedagogy of listening favoured by Reggio Emilia in Italy, which seems an intrinsically democratic approach to pedagogy. Despite this diversity, what connects all social pedagogies is the way of thinking, the philosophy and how values are congruent with the agreed actions. This is known as *haltung* in social pedagogy.

Social pedagogy is delivered by social pedagogues. In Europe, practitioners are often described as social pedagogues underpinned by the principle that learning, care and upbringing are fully interconnected elements of a child's life. They describe their approach as being concerned with the whole person and they refer to the importance of bringing their whole self to work. This is described as the 'three Ps': the professional, the personal and the private (ThemPra, 2018). It is underpinned by the idea that 'every person has inherent potential, is valuable, resourceful and can make a meaningful contribution to the wider community if we find ways of including them'. Stephens (2013) insists that these relationships have to be underpinned by the notion of *caritas*. He argues that *caritas*, a Latin word, is the 'benevolent concern for others that signals a sense of solidarity' (Stephens, 2013, p. 23) and goes further than kindness. This view also informed the work of Loris Malaguzzi (1993), the first head of early childhood provision in Reggio Emilia, Italy. He wrote 'our image of the child is rich in potential, strong, powerful, competent and, most of all, connected to adults and other children' (p. 6).

Social pedagogy in early childhood education begins from the view that early education is a combination of social, pedagogical and political practices and the boundaries between these disciplines must be crossed to provide useful services to children and adults. According to Eichstellar and Holthoff (2011), social pedagogy is concerned with the theory and practice of creating a 'thriving garden for children', creating a fertile self-sustaining ecosystem connecting the child's well-being and learning and resources to their surroundings. Social pedagogy is essentially concerned with well-being, learning and growth (ThemPra, 2018). Eichstellar and Holteff (2011) suggest that social pedagogy is fundamentally concerned with four aspects of the human condition through its practice. These are:

1. A multi-dimensional and holistic understanding of *well-being*;
2. *Learning* from a standpoint of the 'competent' or 'rich' child, where education does not impose but facilitates children's capacity to think for themselves;

3. Authentic and trusting *relationships* between professionals and young people that acknowledge and work with both the authoritative and affectionate, as well as retaining a sense of the private;
4. *Empowerment* or promoting active engagement in one's own life and within society, and as such is fundamentally concerned with children's rights and developing the skills for living in a democracy.

Social pedagogy continues to evolve as a pedagogical response that identifies the educational pathways to promote critical consciousness in all children to enable them to respond to societal changes that affect the relationship between the individual and society especially when there are risks of fragmentation and social exclusion. The story of social pedagogy will therefore continue to be shaped by social pedagogues who courageously embrace a level of pedagogical fluidity that is driven by continual discussion and reflection as we observe and understand the changing world faced by our children.

Why should social leaders support social pedagogy?

Recently, the language of pedagogy has become more common to describe the way we think about delivering ECEC; this is particularly true in some global contexts where educating and caring for the youngest children has tended to be divorced from conceptualization of 'pedagogy'. There are several definitions of pedagogy, particularly over the past twenty-five years when many governments have been keen to introduce their preferred pedagogies to drive their social, economic and political agenda.

The concept of education and learning is integral to pedagogy although we need to be alert to the inclination of modern policymakers and some educationalists to narrow and compress the meaning of education and learning into the schooling and knowing and learning 'stuff' especially in the UK and the United States. Paulo Freire (1968/1999) famously referred to this rote and drill learning as the banking model of education, in which learning is seen in terms of making deposits of knowledge which can quickly descend into treating learners like objects, things to be acted upon rather than people to be related to.

Social pedagogy challenges this perceived reductionist approach to pedagogy acknowledging that pedagogy includes education in its broadest sense, which means a deep engagement with a child's whole upbringing (Petrie, 2020). It is a pedagogy which fits within the concept of regular activities and organizational behaviour and depends very much on the context or setting. Cameron and Moss (2011, p. 88) suggest that:

> *Social pedagogical methods and approaches are constructed in a specific context of the everyday organisation and relational work which takes place with the children.*

Social pedagogy is framed by relationships and social context. Social pedagogy is therefore closely related to society and reflects cultural attitudes and traditions including attitudes to modern childhood and children's upbringing, the relationship between the individual and society, and how society supports its disadvantaged or marginalized members.

Describing ECEC within a social pedagogical framework is not commonplace in many parts of the world, including the UK from where we write. Cameron and Moss (2011) commented that Reggio Emilia fitted the social pedagogical concept but the director, Carlina Rinaldi, rejected this saying she was uncomfortable with being put in an *ism*. Anders (2015) noted that the relative effectiveness of different pedagogical approaches in early childhood has raised substantial debate to try and ascertain the most suitable pedagogy but there is no conclusive evidence to suggest that a single model leads to better educational outcomes for children. Consequently, most countries use a combination of theorists and approaches and adjust and improve the pedagogy as they learn more about how to respond and adapt to the positive and negative elements of their world. As Bruner (1996, pp. 44–65) wrote: 'pedagogy is never innocent' since 'it is a medium that carries its own message' (p. 63). Pedagogy needs to be updated, recreated and renovated within the changes of the new times, otherwise it loses its function and education will not be fit to support children as they navigate rapid social change and anticipate the unfolding future. Pedagogy is never about reproducing an educational model.

Social pedagogy is therefore a set of ideas based on the values of humanity, which are continually reviewed and refreshed by thinkers and practitioners with a shared ethos and set of principles who refine their pedagogical responses to changing social issues with the ultimate intention to create a more just society through educational means. Eriksson (2014) has suggested that trying to define what social pedagogy is may not be the most productive approach and it might be more helpful to ask: 'What can social pedagogy do?'

Social pedagogy is characterized by a humanistic and democratic approach where the individual's own abilities are recognized and acknowledged through respect, dialogue and debate. Social pedagogy offers a framework for professional practice that is based on both formal knowledge of sociology, cultural studies, psychology and so on, and communication, organizational and creative skills including the skills required to work between theory and practice and with the personal and professional.

ThemPra (2018) describe the purpose of social pedagogy as being focused on the well-being, learning and growth of every person underpinned by the view that everyone has potential and can make a valuable and meaningful contribution to the wider community but only if we find ways of including them. Madsen (2005, p. 12) describes this part of social pedagogy as 'spacious' where there is room in society for everyone, regardless of their social, cultural background or their learning or special needs. He argues that the basic justification of social pedagogy is the adoption or acceptance that people live in different worlds, but that we can create conditions so that people can live differently in the world. Therefore, by raising individuals' own awareness of their abilities and responsibilities based on their experiences, they can develop their own identity but with that change better understand their own views, attitudes, self-awareness, tolerance and respect for other people's differences. Social pedagogy is a practical approach and while ECEC can be overwhelmed with policy initiatives, social pedagogy helps because social pedagogy is more concerned with how and why a particular action is taken and relies on building relationships with colleagues to support policy interventions and convert them more quickly into value-led practice.

The LEYF pedagogy provides us with a case study here because it was designed to ensure social purpose was driven through every element of the social business model that could provide a service to children from all backgrounds, but where at least one-third of the places were subsidized for children from disadvantaged backgrounds. Social pedagogy seems a natural framework to develop the pedagogy not least because it offered a practical means of converting our values into action.

How does social pedagogy strengthen social leadership?

Social leaders consider social pedagogy in ECEC as a combination of social, pedagogical and political practices and the boundaries between these disciplines must be crossed to provide useful services to children and adults. For social leaders this is essential to how they deliver a strong social pedagogy which is aligned to the values and ambitions of the organization and supports a culture of well-being and empowerment and strong empathetic relationships.

Case Study
LEYF's social pedagogy

Over ten years ago, I developed what we call the LEYF pedagogy, which was a framework made up of seven strands, each of which were significant to the overarching aim of providing children with the strongest interconnected support to develop and learn. In designing the pedagogy, I sought the input of colleagues because I realized that a pedagogy would need to be shaped within a clear set of values and principles, framed by theoretical ideas and concepts of philosophers, educationalist, psychologists, poets, artists and early years thinkers and be underpinned by an agreed image of the child and how she learns and develops so that we create a relevant and ambitious art, craft and science of ECEC teaching.

The LEYF pedagogy fitted very comfortably within the concept of social pedagogy and our ambition to support people's well-being and happiness, recognizing everyone's intrinsic worth and ability to reach their full potential. As Hamalainen (2003) describes it, we have always been committed to 'promoting people's social functioning, inclusion, participation, social identity and social competence as members of society' (p. 76).

The guiding ethos of social pedagogy anchored the social purpose and the values of LEYF despite the many changes and shifts we implemented to develop a workable model. The LEYF pedagogy, in the spirit of social pedagogy, is dynamic, creative and process-orientated rather than mechanical, procedural and automated and this pedagogical fluidity has shaped our approach as we discover more about children's development and adjust to the changing context of their lives. The pedagogy is built on an understanding of knowledge as something in constant movement. It assumes that a connectivity between thinking and doing is of crucial importance to respond to social challenges (Oliveira-Formosinho and de Sousa, 2019). We were also influenced by the social pedagogy head, heart and hands approach to practice led by people who understand and were willing to share their professional, personal and private selves with the organization for the good of the social purpose. The resulting LEYF pedagogy is made up of seven interwoven strands, each one made from thousands of threads, all of which combine to form a strong learning rope which supports children, families and staff.

The role of the staff aligns very much to the social pedagogy approach where the curriculum is designed to support children to develop across the life course which includes family and the wider community rather than the narrower focus only on learning targets laid out in the UK but also

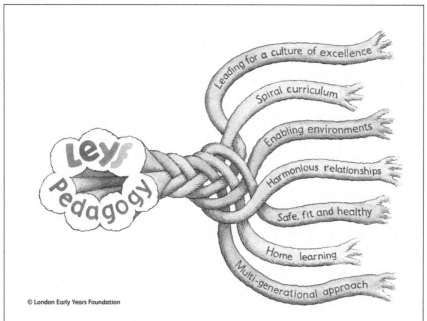

© London Early Years Foundation

Figure 2.1 LEYF Pedagogy.

commonplace across the world. The LEYF approach very much sees the ECEC professional as someone who walks 'alongside' the children, teaching, guiding, reassuring and extending their learning. We believe that pedagogies that are tightly linked to social purpose provide educational pathways to promote academic excellence for all children.

As a social enterprise created to support all children but especially those from disadvantaged backgrounds, we have developed a pedagogy that gives the child and the adults a strong voice and rejects the often deficit position associated with settings focused on the poorer and more deprived communities. This is a pedagogy underpinned by children's rights and participation.

There are three ways that social leaders use social pedagogy to strengthen their leadership. Firstly, it helps them create a culture of well-being and empowerment which reinforces the importance of the social purpose throughout the organization. Secondly, social leaders use the social pedagogical approach to develop staff to be reflective and empathetic which is key to securing the social purpose. Thirdly, social leaders use the principles of social pedagogy to open a wider debate about the purpose of education and how we need to rethink modern ECEC policy in so many parts of the world.

Create a culture of well-being and empowerment

Social leaders use social pedagogy to foster the idea that knowledge is a constant dance between thinking and doing which is of crucial importance if we are to respond to social challenges (Pascal & Bertram, 2012; Oliveira-Formosinho & de Sousa, 2019). The social leader can foster this by driving action research which is an essential element of social pedagogy and the means of supporting leaders at every level of the organization to reflect, influence and consider the complexity of each situation because in social pedagogy the answer often depends on the context. Social leaders recognize this and develop a self-reflective loop to create a culture where staff can continually both drive and respond to changes and use the emerging evidence to shape everyday practice and reframe their theories within a praxeological paradigm by connecting our head, our hands and our hearts. For many social leaders action research is the space where staff question why, what and how things are done and use these questions to gather evidence to gain a greater knowledge of their impact on the service. In doing this, they build confidence, understanding and the capacity to make constructive changes for the better. Social leaders often use action research to develop a growth mindset among staff enabling them to have the courage to explore the pedagogical fluidity that is driven by continual discussion and reflection as we observe the changing world faced by our children. In social pedagogy this space is also called the *common third*.

A helpful way to think about delivering social pedagogy is to consider the role of the head, hands and heart in practice. The head describes the importance of reflection and how social leaders assess their work in the light of theory and self-knowledge and use their learning to make decisions about taking the work forward according to the best interests of children and staff and families. It is also about the power of influence and how social leaders must stand up and be heard, but also sit still and listen deeply to what others have to say. In our dialogues with global ECEC leaders, these 'head' processes were highlighted by Peter Frampton, CEO of the Learning Enrichment Foundation (LEF) in Toronto, Ontario:

> *We've been trying to embed research in our structures and in our work for a good decade now. And it is but not necessarily as a research department. You don't learn without the rigour and you need that academic rigour to influence and to learn for ourselves and it helps staff keep their eye on the ball. It's also a motivator – 'oh my gosh, we're part of this', so it's pride. And it helps people go 'ok, yep, we're measuring resilience'. It has all of these things on the social business side of things, all of these things have multiple impacts. You can justify them from a business perspective, you*

can justify them from an advocacy perspective, you can justify them from a quality perspective. It's interesting how they all interact with each other.

The hands refer to social leaders seeing their work as practical and impacting everyday activities, interactions, relationships and research in a holistic context. Social leaders focus on the 'everyday'. They recognize that what can seem mundane to some is absolutely vital for making a social pedagogy come to life. The small moments in an ECEC setting are where the social pedagogy lies, and so we have to get these small moments right. As Cameron and Moss (2011, p. 88) suggest, 'social pedagogical methods and approaches are constructed in a specific context of the everyday organisation and relational work which takes place with the children'.

Social leaders encourage their staff to bring 'the hand' to work by contributing their interests and enthusiasms to the life of the setting. This might be their music skills or ability to garden and share this with the children and colleagues. This supports their underlying emphasis on building equitable relationships where each person whether adult or child is given a voice and empowered to use it through their practice. The underlying assumption is that everyone has a right to be heard and the opportunity to participate and the resulting relationships (which we refer to as harmonious relationships in LEYF) are not just with the children but with team colleagues, parents, other professionals, members of the local community and more recently through defining our relationship with our natural environment. In our dialogues, Nichole Leigh Mosty described the transformative impact that this approach had in the context of the Ösp Playschool in Reykjavik, Iceland:

I had someone passionate about having the garden clean. She was the self-proclaimed garden monitor and nothing went by on her watch! Everything was tip top when she was there. It was her role because it's what she had an interest in. I saw leadership as a collaborative thing. We all had our roles to play, whether it was leading in a particular area or supporting the children with an activity – like leading the clay workshop, or supporting painting outside. Whatever they had a passion in, that's what they were encouraged to lead on.

Social leaders support staff to bring their hearts to their work recognizing and encouraging their contribution as ethical and emotional beings. In social pedagogy this is also known as *Haltung*, which roughly translates as the mindset, values or personal moral codes that shape the way we think and drive our behaviour and attitudes to the world we live in at work and at home, the situations we face, our relationships and how we apply a profound respect for human dignity (Eichsteller & Holthoff, 2011; Charfe & Gardner, 2019).

This is best delivered in a culture of ambition and growth mindset led by social leaders who build optimism, hope and empowerment. Carol Dweck (2007) popularized the concept of growth mindset: the belief that our intelligence and abilities can develop overtime. In contrast, a fixed mindset regards intelligence or talents as unchangeable. Dweck noted that low-income students were twice as likely to have fixed mindsets compared to their more affluent peers yet having a growth mindset is a key predictor of achievement. The importance of thinking big and having ambition for children from more disadvantaged families must begin early. Gorski et al. (2013), in their work about how to cultivate social justice via education, found that a deficit attitude to teaching children from disadvantaged and poor community was commonplace among teachers. Teachers often saw poverty as the result of personal negative attitudes towards education and an unwillingness to work hard. They were surprised to discover that poor people had similar educational aspirations to their more affluent families but believed the structural factors that led to poverty overwhelmed their abilities.

If social leaders are to deliver their social purpose which is most often addressing a level of disadvantage and poverty, then staff need to be truly reflective of their contributions and the impact this can have on ensuring a fair, inclusive and democratic service.

Develop empathetic and reflective staff

Social leaders understand the importance of cultivating empathetic staff. The social pedagogical concept of *Haltung* is central to attracting and retaining staff whose personal and professional values are empathetic and fundamental to ensuring staff who are willing to respect difference when there is no personal experience of an individual's situation.

The social pedagogical pillars of *Haltung* support staff to constantly self-reflect about their values while also compelling staff to check that their *Haltung* is being supported by their actions. As an ethical orientation it encourages staff to 'strive towards understanding people, being respectful and recognising the unconditional value of human beings' (Kaska, 2015, p. 20). This personal empathy attunes us to the needs of individuals while social empathy connects us to the realities and injustices experienced by others. Social empathy involves recognizing the limitations of our viewpoint by walking around in another's shoes and comparing their path with our own. It leads to a shared understanding of our reciprocal responsibilities echoing a principle of democracy. Building systems such as coaching, talent enrichment and development is central to helping staff to understand their own emotional reactions to their work, their relationships and their communication with children and others. Learning carries with it the responsibility for staff to apply their learning in ethical and effective ways. Ed Vainker, CEO of the Reach Foundation in London, emphasizes the importance of this supportive system surrounding the teacher:

> *What has given teachers and leaders the space to grow has been really good instructional coaching, helping people get really good at teaching. And then some fairly focused professional development alongside it, and then not – as I say – not necessarily feeling that people need to serve a certain amount of time before they can take things on and take on more formal roles.*

Social leaders treat staff, parents and children with respect and aim to build security, trust and positive self-esteem through their relationships with other people. Madsen's (2005, cited in Winman, 2020) idea of the 'spacious' society with room for everyone depends on social leaders who can create the conditions for people to be and live differently while still finding belonging. This requires social leaders to train ECEC professionals in the art and science of empathy so they can see other's points of view and life worlds knowing that this will often be different from their own. Nichole Leigh Mosty shares the joy that comes from this way of working and being in the world:

> *I get little goosebumps when I say this. These are my buzzwords. Collaborative communication. You have to be the most effective listener. When you are that listener and you show people cultural humility, where you open yourself up and they see that, they see this sort of vulnerability and this need for you to learn from them.*

As a result, *Haltung* and the use of self is not something that is relevant in a certain situation or only during working hours but is, as Eichsteller and Holthoff (2011) noted, 'a skin and not a jacket' (p. 34). It is not uncommon to hear social leaders talking about how they bring their whole self to work.

As professionals, ECEC staff are aware of their responsibilities towards others, bringing relevant knowledge, skills and attitudes to their tasks. At the same time, they see themselves not as compartmentalized by the context of work but as the whole person who is not afraid to have fun and enjoy shared humour, express feelings, talk about their lives or share interests. The emphasis is on being genuine. They do not split themselves into work and home boxes, although they apply a professional lens to what is shared. Social leaders encourage their staff colleagues to bring all three aspects – professional, personal and private – to their reflective practice understanding how the three inter-connect in the way they form and nurture relationships. This is often described as a strength-based approach with an appreciation of the strong human being; a view of children advocated by Loris Malaguzzi (1993) from Reggio Emilia who first spoke about the 'rich child' in contrast with the 'poor child' and described the child as strong, powerful, competent and rich in potential with tight connections to other children and adults (Rinaldi, 2006).

From a social leadership perspective, this is reflected in the importance of seeing the potential in every person and building their confidence and self-efficacy as they grow into their roles. The challenge is how social leaders can support ECEC professionals to be confident in their own values, judgements and actions and best make use of their most critical resource – themselves (Ucar, 2012). Stephens insists that a compassionate disposition and kind actions are particularly important if relationships are to be sustained. Jacqueline Lamb, CEO of Indigo Childcare in Glasgow, Scotland, very much echoes this compassionate, trusting and optimistic approach to supporting other professionals to develop:

> *I think it was Drucker that said 'the strongest leaders are those that are not afraid to give power away'. And that, alongside a sort of coaching approach, has been – throughout my whole career – my approach to things. It's people centred. It's about recognising the potential in people. It's about believing in the people that are there and supporting them to get to where they want to be and need to be. For me, that's a success. If I can stand on the outside of this organisation and walk away and see it flourishing without me having anything to do with it, my view is that I've done my job. That whole aspect of not being afraid to give power away, allows people to grow and it also means that there's not a dependency.*

Social leaders recognize that supporting professional development is not simply about sending staff on a training course or teaching people to apply a set of pre-ordained methods. Instead, it is about learning to walk alongside the person, just as the original Greek pedagogues literally did, as this encourages a level of critical self-reflection rooted in an individual's practice as well as a philosophical understanding of their own *Haltung*. As Freire (2001/1996) cautioned though, reflection alone is not enough and there needs to be both 'right thinking and right doing' (p. 39). Cleary (2020) also argues that reflection and ethical reflection are part of guided action and help staff qualify their action. This suggests that reflection that does not help staff develop their practice is likely to be ineffective. Kierkegaard (cited in Hatton, 2013, p. 28) asserts that for a person to become self-aware there needs to be critical reflection on their thoughts, feelings and actions:

Knowing when to push, when to let go, what to listen to, and what to ignore – all these skills are based on the profound respect for human dignity.

Social leaders use the power of influence by finding the balance between heart, hand and head, between using our intellect and our emotional intelligence between knowing when to push through and knowing when to yield to others. Influence is the sweet spot in the middle of all these and it is how we tell the story. Alice Sharp, CEO of Experiential Play in Scotland, describes how these different forces shape professionals across the organization:

My staff colleagues are not just loyal to the company, they're loyal to the students as well. They demonstrate integrity for example we will not take students onto the course if we don't think they're able to do it, and we'll counsel them off the course if we think it's not working, we'll always give them a positive destination. We're not just offering a qualification, we're offering a chance for a young person to change their life path. And that is at the core of what we do. And if the staff are not signed up for that, then I don't really want them as part of my staff.

Social leaders use social pedagogy to offer a coherent philosophy, theory and practice relevant to ECEC.

Widening the debate about the purpose of ECEC

Social leaders use the principles of social pedagogy to open a wider debate about the purpose of education and why we need to rethink modern ECEC policy especially in the UK. Social leaders can use social pedagogy to frame a conversation about what we understand by education, something that is beginning to happen here in the UK, led not by politicians or policymakers but by the Duchess of Cambridge and the Royal Foundation's Centre for Early Childhood.

Social leaders need to be willing to stand up for children by speaking out and speaking up. The raft of compelling research from Heckman (2015) to OECD (2019) confirms the importance of high-quality ECEC as a route to the development of equitable societies and long-term prosperity. Throughout this book we argue that every child should be able to access high-quality, affordable ECEC irrespective of their circumstances – an ECEC that will foster the general well-being and development of children and young people and nurture their ability to interact effectively with their environment and to live a good life so both the individual and society flourish.

Social pedagogy offers a space to debate what we understand by our shared understanding of ECEC and how it fits into the national understanding of the purpose and importance of education. Pestalozzi, an early social pedagogue, described education as rooted in human nature where our identity and purpose in life is created through connections to the community, to the natural world and to spiritual values. It was very much a matter of head, hand and heart (Brühlmeier, 2010). Also, relevant here is John Dewey's (1976) description of learning as shaped by experiences generated from involvement and participation, the development of knowledge and the capability to use such knowledge in a certain situation. Dewey defines learning as a social process which is often translated to mean the process of living not just the preparation for future living. He saw learning as deeply practical with the wider purpose of compensating and equalizing social inequalities. Social pedagogy according to Cameron and Moss (2011) has the potential to promote social justice and support inclusion if allied to political and ethical purpose. Fielding (2007) wrote that in a radical school, 'both education and society develop the conditions of each other's mutual growth' (p. 541). Social pedagogy can be used to distinguish such a relationship across formal and non-formal educational provision, whether radical or otherwise.

> It is not just a method to be imported, but also a rich source of inspiration for critical reflection on the role that pedagogical institutions play in our society.
> (Coussée et al., 2010, p. 808)

In brief, social pedagogy is a theoretical field that can illuminate and inform practice and policy intentions. This way of thinking played a significant part in the design of the LEYF pedagogy and how we use a social pedagogy model to give a voice to the children, staff and families. Social pedagogy does not happen because of the methods used but rather as a result of social pedagogical thinking. As Stephens (2013) explains, social pedagogy is best thought about as a lens through which we see the world and our practice.

Operating a social pedagogy requires social leaders to create a transformative space where staff can be open and reflective, willing to listen and understand the power of building strong relationships. They commit to strengthening the voice of the child and developing professional enquiry all within the context of their particular situations. This also means valuing and trusting staff to make decisions that draw on their knowledge and experience through dialogue and reflection.

According to Bertram and Pascal (2019), early childhood policy is going through a time of transformation as policymakers respond to the compelling evidence base which indicates its potential to achieve social, economic, political and educational progress. However, the fragmentation and complexity of the sector and the diversity of providers and funding mechanisms make this difficult, but social pedagogy with its emphasis on collaboration not competition provides a helpful focus because social leaders look for common ground to build bridges and make connections.

> *the quality of leadership of settings is crucial for enabling learning, pedagogy, participation, distributed power, voice, challenge, stimulation, social equity, democracy, community and achievement to flourish in a positive and purposeful climate.*
>
> (Bertram & Pascal, 2019, p. 183)

Finally, to widen the debate, social leaders understand the importance of telling stories. They know that to influence an audience it is important to involve their heart as well as their mind so best to share some emotions and tell an inspirational story. Being surrounded by adults who use their heads, heart and hand to drive their practice as well as being willing to bring their professional, private and personal selves to work provides a great source of stories and generates a wider discussion. Telling genuine stories and demonstrating values-driven practice is key because as Freire (1968/1999, p. 70) reminds us:

> *Dialogue cannot exist in the absence of a profound love of the world and for people … Because love is an act of courage, not of fear, love is a commitment to other.*

Social pedagogical philosophy, practice and moral code reinforce social leaders' need to drive organizations that ensure practice is 'purposeful, with the ultimate aim of supporting growth, development and well-being' (Charfe & Gardner, 2019, p. 13). Ultimately, social leaders see how social pedagogy can build social integration and collaborative relationships which have the potential to support the holistic development of children so they are able to experience and confidently interact with their world.

Conclusion

Social leaders understand that ECEC pedagogies are the way through which social purpose can be realized. If social purpose is the heart of social leadership, social pedagogy is the heartbeat – it is the process through which the social purpose does its work and brings life to the organization. Social pedagogy is a complex and ambitious field of theory and practice, with implications for wider children's services policy and the organization of services. It reflects cultural attitudes and traditions including attitudes to modern childhood, children's upbringing, the relationship between the individual and society, and how society supports its disadvantaged or marginalized members. It provides leaders with a philosophical, theoretical and practical approach to ECEC that addresses the unfairness that results from poverty and disadvantage for children.

Creating a culture of collaborative innovation

This chapter expands on what we mean by creating a culture of collaborative innovation, which is a key driver in social leadership in ECEC. The chapter addresses three questions:

1. Why does collaborative innovation matter as part of social leadership in ECEC?
2. What does collaborative innovation look and feel like on the ground?
3. How do social leaders create a culture of collaborative innovation?

Why does collaborative innovation matter?

Social leaders focus energy on creating a culture of collaborative innovation for three reasons. Firstly, there is substantial evidence, both in ECEC and beyond, to show that collaborative innovation improves quality and problem-solving in organizations. Secondly, collaborative innovation has been shown to strengthen a sense of shared purpose and this is in turn important for recruitment, retention and staff well-being. Finally, collaborative innovation works to build much-needed cross-sector partnerships that raise the profile of ECEC and the standards within it. Each of these reasons is considered in more detail below.

Collaborative innovation to improve quality

Creating a culture of collaborative innovation is important for organizational success. Research conducted in business settings has shown that grassroots collaborative innovation within an organization can support that organization to be more agile and responsive to the needs of society. For example, Guglielmo and Palsule (2014) have found that organizations which create channels of open collaborative innovation improve their performance because they can respond more effectively to challenges as they arise. Competing in today's business world requires organizations that are constantly innovating and are doing this not just on the basis of managers' ideas, but on the basis of everyone's contribution. We can no longer assume that it is a CEO who will have the right idea when it comes to responding to a new challenge. The more organizations enable a distributed rather than a hierarchical response, the more likely they are to be successful.

This is also the case in the context of ECEC, though the measures of quality and the nature of the challenges will be different. Nichole Leigh Mosty, former director of Ösp Playschool, gives the example of designing and monitoring a programme to welcome refugee families to the Ösp playschool and other ECEC centres in Reykjavik, Iceland. She explains that for the programmes to be a success, it was essential that it was not one specific leader's agenda and evaluation that mattered, but rather a collaborative vision and effort:

> *When it comes to welcoming people into our schools and communities in Reykjavik, we think we do things well. But in reality, there's a lot we need to do differently. Our new families come with new needs, and so we must constantly think about how we can do it better. And that's up to everyone. The manager who has designed and implemented the programme isn't actually the best person to answer the question of whether it's working. We need to open up the possibility for others to see the potential for growth and improvement.*

The link between collaborative innovation and quality ECEC provision is supported by the research of Dennis and O'Connor (2013). They investigated how the organizational climate in ECEC settings impacted on classroom quality and children's outcomes. A key aspect of the organizational climate they measured was collaborative innovation in terms of whether teachers felt able to contribute their own ideas and that these ideas were valued and became the source of collective action. They found that organizational climate, including the dimension of collaborative innovation, was predictive of classroom quality and children's outcomes. That is, the organizations that had a more collaborative and supportive culture were also those with more effective child-adult interactions. In fact, organizational climate was a much better predictor of classroom quality than teacher to child ratios. Similarly, an intervention study carried out in Chile by Arbour et al. (2016) focused on the impact of embedding a culture of collaborative innovation as part of a wider professional development programme for ECEC teachers. The researchers found that when the teachers were encouraged and supported to form collaborative teams, working on continuous quality improvement (CQI) together, this made a significant difference to process quality in the work of professionals and to children's outcomes.

Collaborative innovation to build shared purpose

Collaborative innovation also makes a difference because it creates a stronger sense of shared purpose for everyone working in the organization. The stronger the shared sense of purpose driving everyone forward, the more individuals enjoy what they do and the more they take the initiative to do what is necessary for the organization to succeed. Collaborative innovation is an excellent way to connect and reconnect individuals in an organization with a sense of shared purpose.

One of the ways that leaders foster a shared sense of purpose through collaborative innovation is bringing everyone together to review the values, purpose and mission of the organization. Such experiences are important for establishing openness and ownership within the staff team. When Jacqueline Lamb joined Indigo Childcare Group in Glasgow, for example, she found that there were no official values for the organization in place. Rather than impose her own, or interpret those that she felt were around her, she saw this as an opportunity to engage others from the organization in an open conversation about what the values of Indigo should be:

> *When I started here, we didn't have a clearly articulated vision or values. So we did an exercise with all of the staff to explore our values. It was tricky because they weren't used to being consulted like that. I wanted them to be able to see their words in what we'd done. Practically, we ended up with too many values and perhaps some people would say that the words we shared weren't values at all, but I decided to go with what the staff shared. It was essential that they saw their contribution making a concrete difference and felt a sense of ownership over the organisation.*

As Lamb notes, collaborative activities build shared purpose, even though the outcomes might not be as polished as they would be if the process was less collaborative. The CEO could have come up with a neat set of 3–5 values that could easily have been 'sold' to others, but instead she prioritized the contribution of her team. Reviewing the values collaboratively was her chance to bring people on board with the most integral aspects of the organization. It is not uncommon for staff to feel unsure of the values that an organization officially has, but if they have been fully involved in coming up with these values – in sharing their ideas through conversation – they not only know the values, but feel a strong emotional attachment to them.

Another way that social leaders use a collaborative approach to build shared purpose is through coaching conversations. Eliana Elias and Barbra Blender, two ECEC coaches working in California, US, explained how the key to effective ECEC coaching was to work collaboratively with professionals, constantly connecting and reconnecting with that strong sense of purpose within:

> *I always start coaching by having the teachers define their own personal vision and mission statement, having them figure out what they want for children and families, what they need and deserve, and making that public. We develop the coaching from them. It's super important to take and draw on the wisdom and words of the workforce and then apply it, and always bringing it back to the children.*

Gill Robinson Hickman and Georgia Sorenson (2013) argue that the true leader of any organization is its sense of common purpose. They call this 'invisible leadership'. If staff feel deeply invested in the purpose of the organization, and if it connects with their own sense of individual purpose, this is what will drive the work of the organization forward. In Blender and Elias's statement about coaching, for example, they recognize that the power for change comes about from connecting individual purpose with a sense of wider purpose. This can only be done meaningfully in a collaborative way since we are asking professionals to bring something deep within them to the dialogue about purpose.

Robinson Hickman and Sorenson argue that a shared common purpose – one that is deeply alive in an organization – is a key player in recruitment and retention. Shared purpose is often the reason that people join an organization, and stay. A survey with twenty-one global organizations and a total of 415 staff members from across those organizations showed that a sense of common purpose was ranked as the most influential reason for joining an organization. It outranked opportunities for professional growth, work environment and relationships with the team. This was the case also for the question 'why do you stay?'

In addition to recruitment and retention, invisible leadership changes how staff feel about working for the organization and what they can contribute. For example, 86.6 per cent of respondents in the survey agreed with the statement that 'my organization's purpose inspires me to contribute my best effort or work'.

Robinson Hickman and Sorenson also argue that invisible leadership is important for encouraging more individuals to develop leadership behaviours and practices. This is because a deep understanding of the shared purpose means that more people within the organization are willing to take action, to step up and the take the lead, guided by the common purpose rather than by another individual telling them what to do.

A key aspect of making invisible leadership work is fostering collective capacity. Collective capacity is the 'increased competency of a group over each of its members acting alone' (Robinson Hickman & Sorenson, 2013, p. 81). Collective capacity can be equated with what we have called in this book 'collaborative innovation'. Collective capacity can be fostered through a culture of team working, individuals training for multiple roles, and the cross-organizational development of members of the organizations (e.g. by visiting other parts of the organization). Through this, members of the organization have a sense of the lived purpose of the organization that goes beyond their individual contribution. This enables them to develop a stronger capacity for self-agency, acting as a leader on behalf of the shared purpose.

Cross-sector collaborative innovation

Developing collaborative innovation is not limited to what happens within organizations. Collaborative innovation is a powerful way to work across the ECEC sector, which is often complex and fragmented. It can also help to connect the dots between ECEC and other relevant sectors such as schools, health and employment. Partnership working is essential in order to raise the status of ECEC and improve the quality of provision.

To offer a practical example, spontaneous pockets of cross-sector collaborative innovation in the UK have created opportunities for more settings to access high-quality professional development. Julian Grenier is the head teacher of Sheringham Nursery School and Children's Centre in Newham, East London. He co-founded the East London Partnership Teaching School Alliance, which has pioneered models of cross-sector collaborative innovation for professional development:

> *What we did in Manor Park is we said to our local providers, 'well look, we can all try and do our own thing with the funding we've got but it's probably really hard for all of us, but if between 10–20 of us collaborated on a single project, we'd get massive economy of scale and we'd learn more from each other and we'd get more impact'. And that was really the inspiration behind the project we did in Manor Park, which was called Manor Park Talks. At that scale, you can bring in really experienced trainers, you can train in big rather than small groups, you can pay for monthly coaching for everyone. We could get the Institute of Education (UCL) to work with us around the evidence base and create the iterative relationship between*

evidence and practice on the ground. So what's needed is that sort of collaborative
work at community level to improve practice, not waiting for someone else to show
us the way.

Making the links between ECEC and other sectors is essential if social leaders are
to make a positive difference to children and families. Professor Nurper Ulkuer,
former UNICEF senior advisor for early childhood development, explains how
important it is to embed ECEC as part of health, social work and education
policy.

health, social welfare, child protection – they all have to come together and create
that integrated service, reaching out to the most vulnerable holistically and
equitably.

In her work with UNICEF, Nurper struggled to overcome resistance to a
collaborative approach and to cascade an understanding of ECEC as an integrated
and holistic service model at the heart of health, families, communities, social
services and so on:

When I started working with UNICEF in Turkey in the 1990s, I had a challenge
in collaborating with health colleagues. Every time I went to them and said 'please
let's start working together with the newborn babies, this is what we could bring',
they would say 'no, we're talking about child survival, nothing about development –
let the children survive first'. We brought in experts who said 'those children who
survive, they don't thrive, because they are poor, they don't have an enabling
environment, they don't have stimulation and so on. So you have to work together,
this is an integrated job'.

The resistance to cross-sector collaboration is not only felt in large-scale
organizations such as UNICEF. It is encountered by ECEC leaders who try to
work across local networks to give the best opportunities to the children and
families they serve. Jacqueline Lamb (Indigo Childcare Group) explained to
us her ongoing struggle to bring a speech and language therapist, employed
by the National Health Service, to work within the Indigo settings in Glasgow,
Scotland. Recognizing the prevalence of speech and language difficulties among
the children and families served by Indigo, Jacqueline was acutely aware of the
difference that an on-site specialist could make.

Another social leader, Chantal Williams, CEO of Stepping Stones in Tasmania,
Australia, talks about the work she has done to build links across the community
in order to best support children and families:

About five years ago, the Minister for Education wanted to develop new child and
family learning centres in the community. We've been part of the development

team, even when it was possible that the centre would include a new daycare centre that would be in direct competition with ours. Luckily for us, that didn't happen. But we've stayed on the development team, talking long and hard about how to make sure the centre serves children and families in the community. We've talked about the bus routes that need to go to the centre. We've made sure that the child health nurse will be there, instead of on the other side of town where families can't get to them because they have no transport. We want to make sure that speech pathologists and occupational therapists are there. We want to make sure that there's adjunct care going on, so that parents can come in and get counselling but they can have their children somewhere for a couple of hours without having to pay for childcare. So even though this would appear to be on 'our patch', we have made sure that what is right for our community comes first.

Social leaders recognize that doing the best by children and families involves connecting with many others in the community and ensuring that you work together to make services as accessible and supportive as possible.

What does collaborative innovation in ECEC look like on the ground?

In this part of the chapter, we turn our attention to how collaborative innovation manifests in the everyday context of ECEC. We are interested in what collaborative innovation looks and feels like and how we can know when it is going on and when it needs to be strengthened. We focus on three manifestations of collaborative innovation in ECEC: (1) grassroots change, (2) warm and non-hierarchical relationships and interactions and (3) diversity and inclusion.

Collaborative innovation manifests as grassroots change

When social leaders grow a culture of collaborative innovation, they will see changes and new ideas coming from the grassroots of the organization. Rather than making all the decisions themselves, they will have created a climate in which everyone is willing to bring new ideas, try things out and reflect openly on what has worked and the next steps to take. Change at a grassroots level might be on a small scale. It might be an apprentice's suggestion that the toddler room needs to be slightly reconfigured because they have noticed that the children keep on bumping into a particular piece of furniture. It could be on a much larger scale. It might be someone working in an ECEC centre attempting to negotiate a new partnership on behalf of the wider organization. Dan Wise, Senior Director of Children and Families at the Learning Enrichment Foundation (LEF) in Toronto, Canada, described how one nursery manager steered a course on behalf of the entire organization that has been sustained to this day:

> *We've got one supervisor, who I was talking to about how to get more children outside more of the time. She didn't know how to do this and she reached out to an organisation in Toronto called Evergreen. She negotiated the heck out of that organisation to get several free professional development opportunities for her own staff. But because she kept talking, she ended up pulling together 60 educators from across LEF! Peter [Frampton, CEO of LEF] and I went to that first training day in Carlton village, and it was pouring rain, and it was a beastly day to be outside, but Evergreen made everyone go outside. Everyone got wet and two and a half years later, the Evergreen folks are still one of our partners in professional development for educators. And would we have found them? Yeah, probably, we probably would've stumbled across them. But the point is that this came from a supervisor, she negotiated, she got us this free training, she introduced us to them, and then we took it from there. And in fact we're working with them now on what are called nature play co-leads: these are some self-identified individuals who wanted additional professional development around being outdoors.*

The opposite of this kind of grassroots dynamism is a permission-seeking culture in which no one feels that they can act without seeking and obtaining the explicit permission of someone 'above' them in the organizational hierarchy. In this context, even when professionals officially have some kind of leadership role – for example, leading the baby room or preschool room in the setting – they still feel that they need to ask permission in order to take any kind of decision, big or small. Lamb (CEO of Indigo Childcare) explained how this permission-seeking culture hemmed in the staff at Indigo before her arrival and continued to dominate in the first months of her leadership. She was shocked to find that room leaders and even setting managers were coming to her office to ask for permission to spend as little as £18.

One of the main contexts for grassroots change described by the social leaders we interviewed was pedagogical planning. Social leaders look for opportunities to distribute pedagogical leadership through professional conversations where staff contribute new ideas to pedagogical planning and develop and share their own areas of pedagogical expertise. Nichole Leigh Mosty, describing Ösp Playschool, talks about the magic of distributing pedagogical innovation in this way:

> *The way we ended up doing it in Ösp was that everybody had a leadership role to fill somewhere. We created open areas where you were in charge of a passion*

project, rather than taking responsibility for a particular group of children or a time of the day. If you were a person that liked to work with clay, then you had the clay workshop and it was yours to make it a success and teach others because you couldn't do it all the time. We ended up having a massive two hours of the day where children flowed wherever they wanted, moving between the professionals' passions. And you'd have all these specialists. They weren't head teachers or anything, they were teachers and they were teaching with passion and communicating to their co-workers and to the children. It went further as well. We had open days with parents and they would come in and learn and be hands-on through these passion projects.

What is important in what Leigh Mosty says is that it is not just about the distribution of tasks but rather about a deeper level of connection with the work and between professionals. Working in this way, supporting collaborative innovation and grassroots change, builds a stronger sense of interconnectedness and wholeness among the team.

Collaborative innovation involves warm and non-hierarchical interactions

When it comes to collaborative innovation, the tone of the interactions between professionals matters hugely. Collaborative innovation depends on psychological safety, which has been found to significantly affect how teams perform together and their capacity to innovate (Edmondson, 2018). Our sense of psychological safety, and therefore our desire and capacity to work with others to problem-solve, depends on how we are treated by others. In her seminal research on 'positive deviance' in organizations, Meyerson (2008) found that interactions between individual staff were integral for creating a context in which individuals were willing to try new things and share what they found. In particular, the most effective relationships between staff and managers were those that minimized hierarchical differences. The managers empowered those they were managing rather than making visible shows of power. They did not 'pull rank' but instead supported those they were managing to demonstrate increased levels of self-determination and autonomy.

At LEYF, warmth and non-hierarchical interactions are a fundamental part of the organizational culture. On a practical level, this was embodied through the tendency of managers at different levels in the organization to get 'stuck in' with the work on the floor of the setting (whether mopping up a spill or holding a teething baby) and to exude approachability. This gives everyone a strong sense of working as a team towards a shared purpose. Here is what some of the LEYF teachers say about it:

> *at the conference I noticed that you couldn't really tell who was who, the managers were some of the most excitable, they were the ones that were enjoying it more than anyone else, you can't really tell the difference.*

> *They get quite involved. [Manager] is always out in the room, she sings to the children with the guitar and she goes on trips with us.*

> *Everybody seems to be quite approachable, there's no looking down on each other. That's how I feel – if I have something to say, I can just say it freely.*

> *I think even when we go on training, when we're getting inducted, we've always been told 'look this isn't a hierarchy, here everyone can contribute ideas'. They actually welcome that, they've always said 'if you see something, if you think something, please speak up. If something's wrong, if something's going well, always say so because that contributes to a stronger organisation'.*

> *I was shocked when my manager came in and she was cleaning the table, she was doing everything, and I was thinking to myself 'you're the manager, you're supposed to be in the office'.*

Feeding into this sense of warmth and equality is the physical environment of an organization and how the space is used. The 'open door' between the manager's office and the rest of the ECE setting is of both literal and metaphorical importance when we think about fostering a culture of collaborative innovation through warm and non-hierarchical interactions. It matters to the LEYF professionals quoted above that managers are not physically separate from everyone else. It is important that everyone – even the CEO – is available and visible 'on the floor' of the learning environment. Getting down low, on a level with the interactions at the heart of ECEC, is a key way that social leaders in formal positions of authority can mark out and maintain a culture of collaborative innovation. The flow out of the office and onto the ground enables a flow back in the other direction. Teams feel more able to enter into the setting office and talk about their experiences with the manager if the manager often leaves the office and gets 'stuck in' with whatever is happening on the floor.

Leigh Mosty also talked about the importance of 'getting on the floor' as a marker of cultural humility in her work both as a playschool director and as an ECEC consultant across Reykjavik. Cultural humility involves shelving your qualifications, experience, perspective, strategy and so on. It means choosing to be in the moment with another professional to lay the foundations for openness and collaborative reflection:

You get down on the floor, playing blocks and listening to what this teacher is doing, this pride that she has in what she's done with this child, even though you might have done the same thing a hundred times. That's cultural humility.

Being on the floor is a physical marker of the humility that social leaders use to support others in opening up. When individuals in an organization carry around their importance and their accolades with them, others close down, as Leigh Mosty describes in her own experience:

The biggest mistakes I've ever made, as a leader, whether it be in consulting or in my school is when I took the approach that I had all the answers. I stripped people of their confidence, to understand themselves and to learn and develop, or the confidence in their strengths and recognising that they already have strengths.

Schein and Schein (2018) write about Leigh Mosty's 'cultural humility' as 'humble leadership', whereby leaders commit to approaching problems with others, rather than feeling that the strategic challenges of the organization are only theirs to address. From the perspective of humble leadership, leading is about relating to others, connecting with others and enabling groups to work well together. It depends on creating the conditions for effective teamwork and an organizational climate of openness and trust.

Collaborative innovation builds on diversity and inclusion

Sometimes when we hear a term like 'collaborative innovation' we can imagine that it only ever looks positive and pleasant. We might imagine a group of people smiling and nodding while they throw ideas onto a flipchart. This is a romanticized vision of collaborative innovation. Genuine collaboration must enable different perspectives to come to the table and be heard. This in turn will lead to inevitable disagreements, challenges and tensions and these are central to moving ideas forward. The importance of diversity for the effectiveness of organizations has been highlighted by Syed (2019) in his influential book 'Rebel Ideas'. He argues that we must proactively seek to build diverse ways of being, doing, thinking and living into our organizations in order to extend what the organization is capable of achieving.

In the context of ECEC, Farini (in press) has looked in depth at the nature of pedagogical planning meetings in Reggio Emilia settings in Italy. He shows how disagreement and differing perspectives are a key aspect of pedagogical planning. The disagreements can either be shut down, for example, by a manager attempting to 'pull rank' and paint alternative perspectives as 'silly' or wrong, or they can become the source of constructive debate and collaborative problem-solving. Collaborative innovation is characterized by effective listening and language that opens up, rather than closes down disagreements. This might mean proactively seeking alternative perspectives, and when there are disagreements, asking questions in order to establish more knowledge and understanding about the alternative ways of looking at the issue. What social leaders do not do – because this would close down collaborative innovation – is resort to traditional transactional roles and relationships ('well I'm the person that gets to make this decision and this is what I think').

When we make a conscious effort to open up to diverse perspectives, staff can share something of themselves and bring a personal dimension to work. At LEYF we invite that personal dimension into the organization. One of the LEYF nursery managers described how she felt able to share what mattered to her in the workplace and with her colleagues:

> *When I think about the LEYF approach to leadership, I see warm, friendly and engaging. I see passionate. What does it look like? I see diversity as well, which is important. I feel as a woman that you can share things, I can email something out, say like a Maya Angelou poem, I can share it with the organisation, and I feel heard. For me it's a kind of female leadership which gives leadership a different feel. It's strong and innovative, and welcomes creativity by allowing risk.*

This is a comment not just on diversity but on inclusion. Inclusion is the extent to which diversity can live, breathe and contribute. Social leaders create the conditions in which all people can make themselves (their deepest selves) heard: organizations where diversity is not just tolerated or welcomed but is proactively sought. In Farini's research, inclusive meetings were those where professionals could bring personal expressions rather than be pigeon-holed into whatever role they filled. Ideas took precedence over hierarchies.

How can social leaders foster collaborative innovation in ECE?

In this final part of the chapter, we explore how social leaders set the stage for collaborative innovation within and beyond the organization. What do they do in order to drive forward a culture of collaborative innovation? We have identified three aspects of the approach that social leaders take as part of this, they: (1) prioritize connection and psychological safety because staff must feel emotionally and socially 'held' to feel able to contribute to collaborative innovation; (2) set up processes that support collaborative innovation in a systematic way within the organization; and (3) consistently push beyond the walls of their particular organization so that they can learn from the wider world and foster connections and collaborations that extend beyond their particular staff team.

Prioritizing connection and psychological safety

Collaborative innovation depends on connection and psychological safety; in turn, it can help to build connection and psychological safety.

How do social leaders create this virtuous cycle of connection and collaboration? Our interviews with social leaders in ECEC highlighted the need for authentic care in the workplace. They explained authentic care as a genuine interest in and feeling for and with those individuals who make up the organization, whether they are the professionals, the children, the families or other stakeholders. Social leaders show that they are genuinely interested in the 'whole person' of everyone moving through the organization. They make the time and space to attune to what these individuals do, think and feel. This kind of authentic care cannot be achieved through particular actions or kindness checklists; they flow from genuine feeling. At LEYF, we make a point of practising kindness. We strive to be genuinely interested in each other and to show empathy. When this is working well, it permeates everything that happens in the organization (for a fuller exploration of kindness in social leadership, see Chapter 1 on leading with a social purpose).

A strong organization with strong social leadership will make it possible for individuals to feel accepted fully (Stodd, 2014). In Chapter 2 on social pedagogy, we talk about this in terms of the three Ps – the professional, personal and private (ThemPra, 2015). An important way to show authentic care and build connection is meeting people in moments of personal difficulty or crisis. Ed

Figure 3.1 Collaborative innovation, psychological safety and connection.

Vainker, CEO of the Reach Foundation, explains that this is a strategy that they use in Reach Academy to build stronger relationships with the families that they work with:

> *We make a point of supporting families in moments of crisis. When we do that, we deepen our relationship with them. Whether it's a housing issue or a domestic violence issue, we support them and trust grows.*

The same approach can be applied to professionals working in the organization, responding to the lives of those individuals outside of the workplace. Alice Sharp, CEO of Experiential Play in Scotland, refers to this as a 'people-orientated culture':

> *We're people-orientated. It's all about the people. My staff's families come first. So if there's a crisis at home that needs to be dealt with, then that's it, 'go'. Whether there's a death in the family or a Christmas pageant, whatever it is, family comes first. That people-orientated culture works for us.*

Authentic care is not just a nice way to be. It has the power to shift the culture of the organization from one of transaction to one of transformation, which feeds into the opportunities for collaborative innovation. In the previous section, we looked at the research of Farini which focused on pedagogical planning meetings and the management of conflict within these contexts. Participative management of conflicts was characterized by environments that welcomed genuine personal expressions – environments that invited the 'whole person' into the meeting rather than asking them to simply perform a role within a given hierarchy. Thus, when we create organizational cultures alive with authentic care, we are laying the foundations for interactions that are open and collaborative.

Authentic care builds psychological safety. In twenty years of research analysing all different kinds of team in action in the workplace, Amy Edmondson (2018) found that the element in teams that made the biggest difference to whether they were effective or not was psychological safety. In the teams where people felt that they were emotionally held and cared for by others, individuals were more likely to genuinely reflect, to make change where it was needed, to correct each other and to innovate. This is echoed in Brene Brown's tranche of work around the power of vulnerability for enabling development and change at an individual and organizational level. When we open ourselves up, we are in a position to grow and learn, and opening ourselves up is more likely to happen in situations where we experience and extend authentic care.

Social leaders may well want to think about cultivating their own capacities for authentic care by *practising* empathy, but simultaneously, they will be striving to create the processes and the systems that foster authentic care at an organizational level. Role modelling is an essential part of embedding culture but it is just one kind of embedding mechanism that can be used to shift culture (Schein, 2016). To give an example of how this might look day-to-day, Professor Julie Nicholson explained how leaders in ECEC can contribute to a culture of care and connection by building five minutes into the start and end of each team meeting which is ring-fenced for relational regulation, that is, emotionally connecting with others. When you offer this kind of structure, you are making an implicit statement about the value of authentic care within the organization. You are also making it clear that this is the work of everyone and not just the work of a single line manager. Of course, you can also do this more explicitly. You can engage your team in a discussion of the organizational values and consider whether care, or authenticity, or kindness has a place within the values. Fostering dialogues around these values acts as a starting point for shaping a culture of authentic care, which – as explained earlier in the section – lays the groundwork for both developmental work and more positive relationships with children and families.

Design your organization for collaborative innovation

Social leaders make the time and space for collaborative innovation to happen. In research with young children, Craft et al. (2013) have shown that there are three pedagogical strategies that adults can use to support children's possibility thinking: making time and space, profiling learner agency and standing back. We can apply this as a parallel pedagogy when thinking about how to support collaborative innovation in the context of the ECEC workplace. First and foremost, social leaders have to make the time and space for collaborative innovation to happen. Then within that time and space, they can work to emphasize the agency and decision-making of others and, over time, quieten their own contributions so that others can thrive and grow.

In the context of organizational leadership, making time and space involves setting up processes and systems that build collaborative innovation into the everyday schedule of people's work. This might be time at the beginning of a meeting for people to share something of themselves and reconnect with the sense of shared purpose. This sets the tone for the meeting, demonstrating actively that this is a chance to connect and collaborate.

Once the meeting is in full flow, there is a need to make the time and space for others' contributions to shine through. This might be a social leader stopping and saying 'what do you think about this?' and calling on individuals in the meeting by name, encouraging them to respond with authenticity. It means responding to what people offer with genuine interest and authentic care and encouraging open dialogue and reflections among the whole team. One of the nursery managers at LEYF explained:

> *It's good for staff to reflect themselves. If you are constantly telling them things, they receive the message in a particular way. But if they can reflect themselves, and identify the problems for themselves, there's a much stronger sense of ownership and accountability.*

In response, the sense of autonomy and ownership among professionals at all levels increases and they are more willing to put ideas forward in the future. One LEYF teacher, early in her career, explained:

> *Sometimes you go to your manager and you ask an opinion and she responds with 'what do you think?', 'how do you think this is going to happen?'. She sends it back to you. She's there to guide but you take the lead … So she's giving you a sense of control of the situation and a strong message that 'you can do things, you can change things'. Then I feel like my opinions and my skills, my knowledge and understanding have been taken into account, and whatever I'm bringing has been appreciated.*

Beyond meetings and conversations, there can be processes that support individuals to put forward their own ideas and develop them in the context of the ECEC setting. Lamb (Indigo Childcare group) does this through what she calls 'the ideas process' (described in more detail in the following Case Study). Through the ideas process, individuals in the organization – at any level – are given a simple structure in which to bring forward their own pedagogical ideas. They can bring this proposal to team meetings or supervisions and it works as a formal invitation for grassroots change.

At LEYF, we do something similar but frame it as action research. Action research can be used at different levels in the organization – from an apprentice interested in growing an area of pedagogical practice, to a nursery manager wanting to spread more sustainability across the organization. Mandy Cuttler, the Head of Pedagogy at LEYF, explains how important action research is to the life and liveliness of the organization:

> *Ideas come from everywhere. It could be a teacher seeing something within their setting isn't quite working and they want to look into change. It could be somebody*

who has been on a training course they thought was really interesting. Somebody might have read an article or seen a TV programme or heard someone speak at a conference and decided they'd like to put it into practice in their setting. For example we rolled out woodwork, it began in one nursery and then we rolled it out across all the nurseries having seen how it benefited the children. Action research is the structured process within which we take those ideas and see what can come from them.

We frame the process as action research to ensure that there is space for reflection. As Cuttler explains, 'we're not just making changes for the sake of it – we need to know that things work and how they work so that we can continue to improve'. Social leaders give people a chance to share their ideas and come up with new ways of doing things, but they also invest in the leadership of others by supporting those same individuals to reflect meaningfully on the changes that they have made happen. This means monitoring the change and gathering the appropriate data – whether it's statistics about children's outcomes or qualitative responses from the children, staff or parents about a change that's come about. The data needs to be interpreted and used to inform future actions.

Case Study

The ideas process at Indigo Childcare Group

When Jacqueline Lamb joined Indigo as the CEO in June 2016, she wanted everyone on the team to feel part of something special and to define for themselves what success would look like. She brought staff together to review the purpose and values of the organization and to think about what these strategic documents really meant to them, in the context of their everyday work. She was determined to increase the sense of ownership that staff had over decision-making in the organization, understanding that this was core to improving not only morale but the quality of what the staff could offer. How could the staff go the extra mile to support children and families living with disadvantage if they didn't have a strong sense of meaning and purpose in what they were doing?

As part of this push for increased ownership, Lamb focused on growing opportunities for collaborative innovation right across the team. She developed a process through which individuals could bring new ideas to the table:

> *We wanted everyone to have the opportunity to identify particular things that were of interest to them and a plan for testing them out. We set out a little business case document that we referred to as the 'ideas process' – so they would put a little blurb about what their idea was and they would then say 'OK, this is what I've found out about it, this is what the research shows'. I use 'research' loosely – it was more about going and just finding out a bit more about what they were interested in and the potential difference it could make to the service. They filled out one page and they could bring that to their manager when they felt the time was right.*

Through this process, staff working in Indigo had an opportunity to feel more invested in the future of the service. They were making decisions that would affect how things were done. One staff member introduced teaching Spanish in the Indigo nurseries. Another suggested yoga, and another introduced pet therapy. These ideas came from the staff's own passions and interests but also their responsiveness to the needs of the children. The professionals are well placed to make pedagogical decisions because they are with the children every single day and are in the best position to collaboratively build a curriculum around the interests and needs of the children.

Time beyond the walls of the organization

Earlier in the chapter, we talked about the importance of cross-sector collaborative innovation – collaboration that extends beyond the walls of the organization and seeks to establish wider partnerships. This can be experienced as a tension among social leaders in ECEC. Leaders often want to spend more time within their own organization, shaping things according to what we think is most important. At the same time, they recognize how important it is to continue to learn by connecting with others and collaborating beyond the boundaries of our immediate work. To deal with this tension, they have to proactively safeguard the time they spend beyond the walls of the organization and encourage staff to do the same.

Social leaders are quick with invitations, whether it is inviting community leaders into their setting to see what is happening or visiting another setting to see what they might learn, or attending conferences and professional networks, and engaging through social media in wider dialogues and debates. This kind of wider involvement requires the investment of time, effort and money and its effects might not be immediately visible. Many settings will consider this a challenge but if they are to be innovative, they need to find opportunities and resources to connect outside their own organizations. Activities including meeting and talking to colleagues from different organizations with other experiences and perspectives are a socially beneficial investment. The reward can be significant because opening up to the wider world builds trust and openness which strengthens the organization creating a trusting relationship loop. Lamb describes the impact of taking members of the Indigo team on a visit to LEYF:

They were so excited, none of them had ever done a flight down to London and back up to Scotland in a day. None of them had ever done anything like that for work. And the energy that they had when they came back – that was so crucial. What it did was it brought alive that sort of vision that I'd been talking about. That visit brought that alive for them. They saw that it was possible and they could then see how we could do certain things up here and the energy and excitement that came from that was unbelievable and they still talk about it now. So I think that whole learning cycle is crucial, that they see they are part of all of that learning from the outside world. It's not about any single person bringing ideas back – it's all of us learning from what's out there.

Lamb's quote highlights the intensive 'identity work' (Henderson, 2017) that emerges for ECEC professionals from experiences such as these. Professionals see themselves differently when they take part in a collaborative project that moves beyond the walls of the organization. They have increased confidence in their own contribution and they recognize that bringing ideas from the outside world is part of ECEC pedagogy and therefore part of being an ECEC professional.

Social leaders in ECEC make a point of learning from other disciplines about how to build connections and capacity in the wider community. Vainker (Reach Foundation) has been deeply influenced by the pedagogy of community organizing:

Working with Citizens UK (a community organizing group) has helped us to get better at listening. We've started to see parents and members of the community taking a much more active leadership role. Our first campaign with Citizens was completely driven by parents and some students. It's been so powerful for me to see that – to see how community organisers can give people that kind of structure, space and support to make themselves heard. It feels really valuable and I'm learning a lot from this.

Alice Sharp (Experiential Play) enjoys connecting with those from the arts and creative industries in order to grow her ECEC practice:

People can get really bogged down in what they do but it's so important to look away from the sector and see what others are doing. I work with a sculptor. He's now an artist in residence at a Bristol nursery but I've asked him to work with many different settings, right down to a tiny family learning centre in a deprived part of Glasgow. I met him on the circuit, but we connected. I thought when I met him, he'll bring a different perspective on what it is to work with children and families and that different perspective means a lot.

These comments highlight how social leaders in ECEC are characterized by their constant growth and learning. Pauline Walmsley, CEO of Early Years in Northern Ireland, explained how this was a key part of her identity and professional life:

Engaging with people, connecting with people. I've always been that sort of person. I'm always interested. My modus operandi would not be to send an email but to lift the phone and talk to somebody and again it comes back to what I said – it's in those conversations that I think you build ideas and I think you build connections and you see the opportunities to do something in partnership. Or at the very least you leave the conversation with a connection, so that if you have a problem in a month's time or a year's time, you can easily lift the phone again and go back to someone for advice.

One of my favourite sayings to the staff – is 'how do we get the story out of the room?'. I think that's important and inculcating that way of thinking among staff – who else needs to know about this? Who else needs to engage? How do we get the story out of the room? Is there anyone else we need to bring on board with this? Those are all really important questions to be continually asking.

Proactively seeking diverse perspectives can prompt ECEC leaders to seek alternative partnerships and points of view among other industries and sectors.

Social leaders seek out the opportunities to connect with and learn from others. They also tend to assume that this is what everyone else wants to do and so they look for the opportunities to make this possible for everyone in the organization. They consistently role model an 'always learning' disposition to everyone they come into contact with. Through this approach, social leaders develop and maintain a culture of collaborative innovation that enables development within organizations and across the ECEC sector.

Conclusion

Social leaders understand the importance of collaborative innovation for improving quality of ECEC provision, building a shared sense of purpose and establishing productive and urgently needed partnerships across the sector. On the ground, collaborative innovation manifests as grassroots innovation where diverse members of the organization can make themselves heard and contribute ideas and perspectives. Integral to this is valuing and supporting warm, non-hierarchical relationships that increase psychological safety in the workplace and enable open and trusting professional dialogues. As well as building this kind of organizational climate, social leaders design systems and processes that support collaborative innovation. This means making the time and space for collaborative innovation processes and committing time to developing partnerships and experiences beyond the walls of the organization, both for themselves and for others in the organization. This is essential because the most productive collaborative innovation processes and projects are inspired through external relationships cutting across traditional boundaries.

4

Investing in others' leadership

This chapter explores the importance of investing in others' leadership as part of social leadership in ECEC. The chapter is structured around three questions:

1. Why does investing in others' leadership matter in ECEC?
2. What does investing in others' leadership look and feel like on the ground?
3. How do social leaders invest in others' leadership?

Why does investing in others' leadership matter in ECEC?

In this part of the chapter, we look at the rationale for prioritizing the leadership development of ECEC professionals across an organization, regardless of their position in any formal hierarchies. We present three key reasons why social leaders need to invest in the leadership of others, supported by research evidence, practice at LEYF and conversations with ECEC leaders around the world. We argue that investing in others' leadership development is important because it:

1. Contributes to raising the quality of ECEC, as numerous studies have found a positive link between leadership culture and quality in ECEC.
2. Supports improvements in recruitment, retention and well-being because leadership development is an investment in the 'whole self' of the professional and this in turn makes work more meaningful and fulfilling.
3. Builds confidence, assertiveness and voice across the sector. This is much-needed among ECEC professionals in order to raise the status of the work that they do and struggle for the rewards they are owed.

We look at each of these factors in more detail below.

The link between leadership development and quality

International research demonstrates a consistent and robust link between the quality of leadership in ECEC, process, quality and children's outcomes. The Organisation for Economic Co-Operation and Development (OECD) has focused increasingly on the quality of ECEC provision, recognizing that only high-quality ECEC has a positive impact on children's outcomes and is particularly important for those children coming from backgrounds of disadvantage. In Douglass's (2019) working paper for the OECD, she highlights the evidence to show that building high-quality leadership improves quality in the provision for children and families.

To explain why high-quality leadership impacts positively on ECEC quality, Douglass refers to a model produced by Strehmel (2016) which outlines the many ways in which leadership influences what happens in an ECEC setting. Strehmel explains how improvements in leadership lead to changes in the setting including increased levels of professional and leadership development among staff, the strength of shared purpose and vision, a positive working environment, staff motivation and the commitment to learning and reflection within the organizational culture. These factors in turn impact on how professionals approach their work and the process quality (i.e. the quality of interactions with children and families) that they can achieve. This model is supported by studies that have shown how the organizational climate, created by leaders, determines the capacity for organizational improvements (Gittell et al., 2008; Gittell et al., 2010; Douglass, 2011; Gittell, 2016).

It is important to note that in Strehmel's model, an essential part of the influence that leaders have is via the leadership development of others. A vehicle for making change within the organization is the extent to which all staff are showing leadership and are developing as leaders. Within Douglass's working paper, she focuses on a subset of research studies that highlight this aspect of the organizational climate and its impact on measures of process quality and children's outcomes. For example, a study by (Arbour et al., (2016) looked at the impact of developing the capacity of staff to use Continuous Quality Improvement (CQI) as part of their practice and build it into the culture of the school. They found that when professional development was complemented by this leadership skill (using CQI), there was a significant positive effect on classroom quality and children's emotional, social and language development. We take this as evidence that investing in the growth of leadership skills and practices (such as CQI) makes a concrete difference on the ground for children and families served by ECEC.

This detailed research evidence is reflected by our conversations with ECEC leaders from around the world and what they noticed in their many years of experience of leading ECEC organizations. For them, there was a clear link between the extent to which their staff were able to show leadership and the impact delivered by the organization. The following description from Chantal Williams, CEO of Stepping Stones in Australia, shows how drawing an individual professional out of themselves and then helping them to find the leader within, has a positive impact on the organizational culture and the relationships that can be developed with children and families.

> *Jonathan's been with us for about 8–9 years. He began with his Certificate 3 which is the one below Diploma. And we really wanted him to do the Diploma. He started it, didn't do much with it and in the end, he dropped it. However, over the past months, Janelle (our pedagogical leader) has been there in Jonathan's setting and she's been working with him to build his leadership skills. Through their conversations, she encouraged him to think more about how the setting could work more with the families it serves, particularly those who speak Arabic and don't have much English. On the basis of that conversation, he took the initiative to teach himself some Arabic. So, he's now the person that communicates with our Arabic speaking families who use that centre. He leads on that. He's come from just wanting to work with the 3–5s, to Jonathan being the one in the forefront if families need some help. And now he's re-enrolled in his diploma, because Janelle has said to him 'you are just so capable Jonathan and we really want to see you keep going'.*
>
> *Janelle has helped him to find these little ways of making a huge difference, and he's just taken off. It's awesome stuff, for him and for everyone.*

The example of Jonathan brings to life the link between leadership development and the quality of provision in ECEC. Social leaders can make a concrete difference to children and families by investing in leadership development across an organization and helping more individuals to find what they are good at and how they can contribute more to the organization and those they serve.

Leadership development supports individuals and organizations to flourish

Chantal Williams's description of Jonathan's emerging leadership highlights another important aspect of investing in others' leadership development: it supports individuals to flourish, which in turn supports organizations to flourish. Leadership development when done well combines personal and professional development, because it involves building a vision that makes sense for both the individual and the collective (Woodrow & Busch, 2008; Henderson, 2017). As individuals, we can only build a vision for ECEC when we look at what matters personally to us: our values. This is why leadership development starts with an exploration of values and a vision that flows from these values.

We explored personal-professional connection in our conversation with Eliana Elias and Barbra Blender, two US ECEC coaches working in California. They described how important it was, when working with ECEC professionals, to start with what was inside.

> *Eliana: We don't approach our coaching with small tasks and skills. Instead, we approach our coaching with concepts that the teachers can apply in different ways. We build something from the inside out.*

> *Barbra: We make it a real point to build authentic relationships and to really take the time – authentically – to get to know the teacher, to understand her values, her perceptions, her beliefs, what she cares about, what she's striving for with the kids. When you ask teachers 'What do you want for the kids? What's important to you? Why does it matter?' They say the most beautiful things. We can do so much by just unpacking that and giving the teacher a voice and truly listening, and documenting their practice in line with this vision.*

What Barbra and Eliana are describing is deep 'identity work' that is written into leadership development for the ECEC professional. While identity work can be deeply challenging, it can also lead to greater levels of fulfilment (Henderson, 2017). When we engage in identity work in the context of the workplace, we are being asked to bring our whole selves, in a state of dynamism, into the organization. We are being asked to share something of ourselves in transition. If, when doing this, we are met with a psychologically safe environment, we are likely to find that our work is much more meaningful as a result of undertaking this identity work. In theories of social leadership in the context of business, Guglielmo and Palsule (2014) and Stodd (2016) have emphasized the role of personal-professional fulfilment in the contemporary workplace. They suggest that individuals simply will not stay with organizations that do not give them the opportunity to develop as whole people.

Similarly, in her theory of feminine leadership, Jironet (2020) suggests that for Generation Z (born 1997 to 2015), their priorities in the workplace are: 'authenticity, growth and a sense of purpose'. According to this perspective, those who have recently joined the ECEC workforce want more than to simply feel financially secure or liked by others, they want to feel that they are developing as a whole person. This perspective is echoed in Schein and Schein (2019) who suggest that the divide between personal and professional needs to be troubled in the working environments across contemporary society. Employees need to feel that they can appear and develop as their whole self and this can be achieved through leadership development. If the perspectives of these business theorists are right, an investment in leadership development as part of social leadership would help to bring more, much-needed, well-being in the ECEC workplace (Cumming & Wong, 2019).

Professionals working in LEYF describe this interweaving of professional and personal development:

You feel that actually I'm part of this, you know, this is LEYF but I'm LEYF as well so I can contribute to make LEYF great, to help the children, to give the children a better life, a future, to make a foundation for them.

I haven't worked in lots of organisations, but when I look back at where I have worked and I talk to staff that come in from other organisations, I realise that there is something quite different here, and it is a different experience working here … and it makes the job interesting, stimulating and it really does make it fulfilling.

I've been in nurseries since I was 17 but I find that even now I'm still learning new things, which is really good so it doesn't get boring, you're not stuck in one learning place, you actually keep moving. I mean I know a lot of people do get stuck in one place, and they're just in that rut, but I find that every day I'm learning new things and colleagues at LEYF challenge me to take the chance, to go ahead.

Social leaders invest in others' leadership development because it is an investment in people more broadly. The skills and behaviours that individuals develop through a leadership focus will improve directly on quality, but there is also this important indirect effect, whereby leadership development influences how staff feel and what they are willing to give of themselves. This concretely matters for recruitment (how much will staff recommend the organization as a good place to work?), retention (how long will staff want to stay with the organization?) and effectiveness (will they want to go the extra mile to support the organizational purpose and ultimately the children and families you serve?). The knock-on effect on the child is articulated clearly by the professionals at LEYF. They are well aware that their own sense of fulfilment, as whole people influences what they can offer to children:

if the employee is happy and fulfilled, and the environment is supportive and dynamic, the children can feel it, and they feel more relaxed and they're happy and that has a huge impact on the way that they feel as well.

If you feel comfortable and you come to nursery in a positive way, then obviously the children will feel positive and motivated too. But if you come in the nursery and you're bored, and you're thinking you're just at work, not really having the motivation for anything, they will see and they will imitate that.

When you feel that you are valued, I really think that has a lot to do with your impact on the children. You are encouraged to do more, you have an open mind to do better things, because you are not just left behind.

By investing in others' leadership development, social leaders build an organizational culture in which everyone is learning and growing as whole people, and this includes both the professionals, the children and their parents.

Leadership development to build a stronger ECEC voice

In many parts of the world, the ECEC workforce is downtrodden and must grow a stronger voice in order to demand changes to the conditions of work and the status of ECEC as a profession. Developing leadership in ECEC is a fundamental way to build advocacy and activism on behalf of the sector (Woodrow & Busch, 2008). When individuals develop their leadership capacities, they are better able to tell their own story with confidence and in doing so, better represent the sector and call for much needed investment and support.

Many ECEC professionals are poorly rewarded for the essential service they contribute to society. An OECD (2018) report across eight countries showed that while ECEC professionals show high levels of satisfaction with their chosen work, they were much less satisfied with the conditions in which they worked. Most ECEC professionals are not satisfied with their pay and they were concerned about the lack of progression routes within ECEC. Professionals, across those eight countries, report feeling stress as a result of the imbalance between what they were being asked to contribute on a daily basis and the level of reward that they were receiving. To put this in context, a report by Bonetti (2019) focusing on the ECEC workforce in the UK shows that ECEC professionals are paid almost as little as retail workers and in some parts of the sector, ECEC professionals are actually paid less than retail workers. This has led many to suggest that a workforce crisis is imminent, since maintaining recruitment and retention will not be possible given those conditions. Others argue that the workforce crisis is already upon us (Early Years Workforce

Commission, 2021). Although the conditions for ECEC professionals in the UK are shocking, this issue is not isolated to a single country and it is the case in many national contexts that there is a lack of recognition for the contribution made by the ECEC workforce. Social leaders cannot shy away from this stark reality and the social leadership approach must be part of a solution to these problematic circumstances.

Social leadership involves growing the voice of the sector by investing in leadership broadly. The identity work of leadership development, outlined in the earlier sections, brings with it new ways of seeing the world, including the injustices in the ECEC system and the policies that underpin it. Blender and Elias explain this as an important dimension of the coaching work they do:

> Barbra: *The work we do can be validating to the workforce. They say 'oh yeah, I know that something didn't feel quite right and now I'm naming and I'm seeing it'. It can be distressing for them to realise the injustice of the system. We just try to hold those perspectives and help empower them on what they want for themselves.*

> Eliana: *I have a lot of teachers who are now taking on advocacy roles, going to meetings, participating in the larger scale. We have a strong group of family childcare providers that I have worked with who are now pretty powerful advocates in the city and really understand the system.*

Advocacy training then becomes a key aspect of leadership development and this, in turn, can become a means for making real urgently needed changes in the ECEC sector. Chantal Williams, CEO of Stepping Stones in Australia, offers us an example of how this growing professional voice can assert itself and make a real difference. She described a situation when she and her colleagues joined forces with other professionals to successfully challenge a move by local government in Tasmania to move children into school provision at a younger age. The group successfully lobbied for a local government pilot to support more children entering ECEC, rather than school provision. In this case, the professionals were convinced this was the best solution for the children supported by their families – and, most importantly, they had the leadership capacities to speak up for change.

The connection between leadership development and a voice for the sector is explored in more depth in the following case study, focusing on the approach taken by the team at the Learning Enrichment Foundation (LEF) in Toronto, Canada.

Case Study

Leadership development and voice among ECEC professionals at the Learning Enrichment Foundation in Toronto, Canada

The Learning Enrichment Foundation (LEF) supports thorough leadership development among their ECEC teams. Dan Wise, Senior Director of Children and Families at LEF, explains how this leadership development is an essential part of building the identity of individual professionals around their essential contribution to society and raising the status of ECEC:

> *One of the first things that I did when I started going to team meetings is to be really clear that everyone needed to think about themselves as educators. We've tried through our professional development approach over the past four years to build on that and also to help professionals to communicate this identity to others as well.*

Peter Frampton, CEO of LEF, explains that the message needs to be consistently reinforced. He explains:

> *We publicly say to everyone that while teachers impart knowledge, early childhood educators lay the foundation for life and for learning. So, let's not make any mistakes about who is more important. And it's about reinforcing that message not just among ourselves, but out there in the public. So when you're holding meetings, you're running a conference, you're meeting politicians – it's always the same message. Elevating the role is huge and it will take decades, but it's not just because it makes LEF stronger, it's just got to change.*

Katrina Estey, Director of School Age Children, describes how growing this strong voice is closely linked to building leadership among the educators. For her, the shift comes when educators can show more agency as part of their everyday work and can lead the decision-making and initiatives that they know are needed:

> *We've used coaching conversations as the key way to unlock that leadership development. Supervisors at the beginning were coming to me to ask about the decisions they should make, and I was turning it back round to them and saying 'I don't know, you know more about the context, so what do you think?'. And it's the same now for the educators. They might come to their supervisor to ask about a decision and what they should do, and the supervisor will support them to work out the next steps for themselves. It builds leadership and confidence.*

In addition to this job-embedded professional development (JEPD), LEF access leadership development through the Social Enterprise Academy certification programme. In fact, when they first started sending members of the team onto this programme, they chose to focus on ECEC professionals rather than more senior figures within the organization. Dan explains:

> *We didn't start – intentionally – with the senior team. We started with the supervisors of the individual centres. So, they had information about how to be a leader, how to think about decisions, how to have the courageous conversations, how to understand different leadership concepts and theories before the senior team did and that was very intentional so that they could begin to make their own decisions. Now we have some of the senior team and some of the educators doing it. Some of the educators might say to me 'well I don't lead anything', but that's where we need to draw out their reflectiveness. So I'll say 'but you're in the preschool room aren't you? And what are you doing in that room?'. They'll explain it to me and I'll say 'well that sounds like leading'. I remember a conversation with a particular educator, and after I challenged her to see this, she sat up straighter in her seat, and she said 'oh well I've never thought of that before'. And so again it's about reinforcing the fact that you are already a leader and in fact you're doing way more exciting leadership work than I am. 'You've got a bunch of eager pre-schoolers or toddlers or babies that look up to you and you are leading them, so don't ever underestimate what it is that you are doing. You are leading.'*

Peter emphasizes again the importance of sending supervisors and educators on the leadership development programme, before senior management:

> *Our frontline supervisors taught our senior management what they had learned for two years before the senior managers got to do the programme. That was a really clear message. No, you guys matter more – and in doing that teaching, it reinforced the learning. So it's had a remarkable impact.*

What does investing in others' leadership look like on the ground?

Having established that broad leadership development matters for quality, recruitment, retention, well-being and voice in the ECEC sector, we consider two main ways to invest in others' leadership as part of social leadership in ECEC. Firstly, we focus on how social leaders distribute leadership roles across the organization and encourage others to step up and take on more leadership responsibility. Secondly, we highlight coaching as a key method for leadership development across ECEC organizations.

Distributing leadership responsibilities

Social leaders invest in the development of others by distributing leadership responsibilities across the organization. They look for opportunities to bring others into leadership roles and challenge individuals to move beyond their comfort zone when it comes to leading. More broadly, social leaders foster a climate in which people can demonstrate leadership behaviours regardless of the roles they fulfil.

For Nichole Leigh Mosty, former director of Ösp playschool in Reykjavik and now Icelandic politician, social leadership is about findings ways to share responsibility, professionalism and decision-making:

> *It's a really easy for a centre leader to have in their hand an A-Z compendium on how to do every single thing that happens in the centre, even down to changing a diaper. But it's not good enough and it doesn't work in the long-term. Teachers need to be empowered to work out things for themselves. If you're going to build a house where everyone develops and learns, you can't have leaders that like to hoard responsibilities and skills. Hoarders repel people from the vision, from wanting to take a part and having their own initiative. You have to build the house with lots of space for collaboration, reflection and community leadership.*

Social leaders look for opportunities to draw more people into decision-making. Even when they have their own feelings about how something should happen, they are prepared to open up processes in order for others to have a say and a chance to demonstrate and develop their own leadership. In Chapter 3, we looked at the example of Jacqueline Lamb involving everyone in Indigo Childcare Group in coming up with the organizational values. Framing this experience, Lamb quotes Peter Drucker, classic management theorist, in explaining that strong leadership is about the willingness to give power to others to support the growth of others and to avoid a culture of dependency and permission-seeking.

Ed Vainker (Reach Foundation) also looks for opportunities to give people more leadership responsibility, regardless of how long they have been with the organization or how young they are:

> *It's a core part of what we do that we don't need professionals to serve for a particular amount of time before trusting them with a leadership role. If they know they're up to the challenge, we trust them.*

Social leaders also know when to push professionals to go beyond their comfort zone in order to develop their leadership capacity. At LEYF, there is a strong culture of continuous growth and improvement and this applies to individuals' professional and leadership development as well. Nick Corlett, Senior Nursery Manager and Sustainability Lead at LEYF, explains how this culture runs through the organization at every level:

We have an encouraging, team-based culture here. We want new ideas to come from teachers and room leaders to the deputies and managers. If you are an apprentice, and the Apprentice Manager sees that little spark she will say 'you did that really well and I can see you enjoyed that; have you spoken to your manager about it?' She is part of that encouraging process and will ensure the Manager knows about the apprentice's success so she can nurture it and develop it further. It's very much about inspiring and working alongside one another and the apprentice can lead because we need to nurture that passion. So we're very big on 'you did that really well and I think you should do this for us …' and that very obviously cascades down from June. For example she will notice an interest and remember it and then find a way to nurture it whether directly or through the organisational learning processes. If the CEO says I can do it, and believes in me and gives me the chance then of course I can do it. I am now the LEYF Sustainability Lead because she noticed my interest and nurtured it.

Professionals in LEYF echo this sense of constant learning opportunities and challenges and invitations to step forward and lead in new ways:

I started on the preschool room but when someone left from the baby room, they encouraged me to go for the room leader role in the baby room. I wasn't sure but the manager said 'no you can do it'. They reassured me a lot and encouraged me to go for the role. Since getting it I have been given lots of leadership and coaching training to support me to do well in the role.

Internal vacancies are advertised before they are advertised externally and you are really encouraged to apply. They'll say 'why can't you try this?'. They want to boost your career which is really nice. Here we are really encouraged, and supported to push your career to a limit.

Distributing leadership, as part of social leadership, is not just about dishing out responsibilities and roles from the top. It is about creating a culture in which people can come forward with their own ideas, decisions and initiatives and have the capacity to make these happen. Meyerson (2008) writes about this as 'positive deviance', which is the innovation that professionals bring regardless of their role or experience within an organization. This innovation can either be supported and enabled to flourish, or it can be squashed. Social leaders support positive deviance by creating relationships and interactions that encourage individuals to think for themselves and to try and do things differently if they think it will serve the common purpose more effectively. According to Leigh Mosty, this is about setting the scene and asking the right questions to draw people into collaborative leadership conversations:

> *They have to believe that you're open to giving them a part of that success. You're saying ok we're going to make this school great, you and I. We're going to do it together. How can we do it?*

According to Meyerson's (2008) research, some organizations are better than others at supporting positive deviance to flourish. There are two main characteristics of organizations in which positive deviance can take root and drive improvement. Firstly, positive deviance is supported by the relationship that individuals have with others in the organization, and particularly their manager. When managers minimize differences in power and hierarchy, and create space for open and equal dialogue, individual professionals are more likely to show positive deviance. On the other hand, when managers 'pull rank' and rely on overly traditional formal management procedures to keep people 'in line', positive deviance will wilt. The second characteristic of organizations that help positive deviance to thrive is that they find ways to share the 'small wins' of positive deviance. Leaders within the organization will spend time looking for examples of positive deviance and when they find them, they will share them across the organization. In the example of the professional who brings in some flowers to the setting, a manager might notice this and take a photograph of the children interacting with the flowers and post it on internal social media describing the impact this has had on the children. Building on these lessons, social leaders invest in others' leadership by building warm non-hierarchical relationships between professionals, including in line management, and spending time looking for the 'small wins' of positive deviance and sharing these across the organization.

Coaching

Leadership development as part of social leadership is underpinned by the use of coaching throughout an organization. In the case study below, we highlight the different ways that social leaders in ECEC talk about the potential of coaching and how they use it as part of their practice.

In their review of professional learning in ECEC around the world, Rogers et al. (2017) conclude that coaching can be an important aspect of effective professional development programmes. Professional development was most effective in improving outcomes for children when it combined structured input (e.g. through workshops) alongside coaching that would help to embed the pedagogical practice highlighted through the input. Coaching was important for sustaining and growing change, and it seemed to be most effective when it focused on specific goals relating to a particular area of practice.

Coaching is powerful because the starting point for any coaching process is the choice and perspective of the person being coached. It therefore heightens agency – an awareness of how you can act on the world around you and a willingness to take action. Coaching is about building your own vision, setting your own goals, making choices for yourself and stepping up. While more traditional forms of professional development (e.g. one-off training days) can lead to high levels of individuals 'zoning out' or failing to make or sustain concrete changes in their practice, the intensity of coaching makes this more unlikely. In a coaching situation, the spotlight is on the professional to work with their own resources to make, monitor and refine changes in practice. It is also a context in which the personal and the professional are much more likely to meet, for example, by opening up dialogues about an individuals' values. Values impact on our professional practice but emerge from a personal place. Because of this personal dimension, thinking about and planning our actions in relation to our values can lead to deeper shifts in practice that are more likely to stick.

Of course, as with anything, coaching can be done badly. It might be too prescriptive or not structured enough to support development. Individuals might feel too under the spotlight and clam up as a result. Even if it's done well, it is expensive given the personal connection necessary from the one to one nature of coaching, regardless of whether it is face-to-face or online. This is why many social leaders will focus on building a coaching culture within the organization, so that coaching conversations become the norm and central to how the organization operates rather than something special and external. This is exemplified in the following case study.

How do social leaders invest in the leadership of others?

In this final part of the chapter, we look at how social leaders enable leadership development across ECEC organizations. We look at three key aspects of this: (1) social leaders' prioritization of JEPD within organizations, (2) their

Case Study
Embedding coaching in ECEC organizations

Social leaders do not treat coaching as something 'special' to add on to the everyday working environment. They seek to embed a coaching culture within the ECEC organization, so that individual growth and learning is just a part of the 'usual business'. The following comments from ECEC leaders around the world highlight the importance of this.

Throughout my whole career, coaching has been my approach. It's people centred. It's about recognising the potential in people. It's about believing in the people that are there, and supporting them to get to where they want to be and need to be. For me, that's a success. If I can stand on the outside of this organisation and walk away and see it flourishing without me having anything to do with it, my view is that I've done my job.

(Jacqueline Lamb, Indigo Childcare)

Conversations with the pedagogical leader are key. Staff don't have any time off the floor – she doesn't take them away and instead sits with them and says let's make a plan. These are just quiet gentle conversations, gentle pushes, gentle suggestions and then helping them scaffold where they want to be. The professionals here have always got someone championing them and their learning, and they know that.

(Chantal Williams, Stepping Stones)

Instructional coaching has been really important for us all the way through. Every week someone comes and watches you do your job and gives you an action step – a bitesize manageable piece of feedback. And everyone in the building has that. That's not a deficit 'I'm struggling' kind of thing, it's for everyone. I think that has helped people to get better at their job more quickly and helped people to take on more responsibility.

(Ed Vainker, Reach Foundation)

We have invested heavily in a mentoring and coaching approach. All of our managers are trained as mentors and coaches. We use it internally and also use it in our approach as early years specialists with the sector and the settings we work with.

(Pauline Walmsley, Early Years)

When it comes to leadership, we have this idea that authority is given. It's not. It's assumed. And so part of the trick is to assume that they [ECEC professionals] have the authority in the first place. So the coaching conversations help get them there, to that place where they assume their authority. You're asking people to be vulnerable because vulnerability is the greatest sign of strength and it is what is absolutely required for an entrepreneurial and social change mindset. But if you're going to ask people to be vulnerable, you've got to back that up with the right training and coaching. You've got to help them to get there.

(Peter Frampton, Learning Enrichment Foundation)

work enabling everyone, regardless of hierarchies, to own leadership and understand what it looks like day to day and (3) their commitment to drawing out leadership potential particularly through the use of action research.

Social leaders take professional development seriously

There's no question that social leaders are committed to helping everyone, child or adult, fulfil their potential. They know that ECEC is all about growth and learning, and that this is just as true for adult professionals as it is for the children and the families served by ECEC. They invest in others' leadership on the basis that everyone can show leadership. The leaders we interviewed spoke with passion and conviction about developing their teams. They recognize that ECEC is a project that involves meeting the developmental needs of children, families *and also* the professionals that serve these children and families. As Leigh Mosty so eloquently explains: 'ECEC centres are the place where the whole community comes to develop.'

Because of this commitment, social leaders spend a high proportion of their own time working on professional development initiatives and programmes that can be embedded in the organization. They see this as a key aspect of their role. They recognize the gaps in leadership development within their teams and seek practical ways to address this. For example, Jacqueline Lamb saw a gap in the leadership behaviours shown by the room leaders within the daycare settings at Indigo Childcare Group. In response, she developed a bespoke training programme specifically for room leaders so that they can take their practice to the next level and impact positively on the whole organization.

When there are limits on budget, as there almost always are, social leaders think creatively about professional development and how the same needs can be met when the resourcing is far from ideal. This might involve looking for ways to embed professional development into the day-to-day working context such as Chantal Williams's explanations about how the pedagogical leader can coach others through gentle conversations that happen 'on the floor' while professionals are working. LEYF employs pedagogy mentors who work in companionable partnership with teachers, using a coaching conversation to deepen pedagogical confidence. Such JEPD happens on-site part of practice, and is gaining increasing levels of attention (Boud & Hager, 2012). However, researchers in ECEC do warn that in order for JEPD to be effective it cannot simply be the 'cheap' option. It requires money, time, energy and expertise if it is to make a difference (Whalen et al., 2016).

To increase opportunities for professional development, social leaders often partner with others across the sector through reflective exchange programmes where they visit other settings to learn from them. In Chapter 3, we saw how the East London Research Schools Partnership was able to greatly boost their professional development by coming together as a cluster of settings. As a result of this partnership, they could afford to increase the amount and intensity of the developmental opportunities on offer. Pauline Walmsley's passionate commitment to professional development among the team at Early Years is the focus of the following case study. As you will see, when there are limits on budgets, Walmsley has used cross-sector projects as a way to enhance professional development, particularly by partnering more experienced individuals with their less experienced colleagues.

Social leaders support others to own leadership

Social leaders are committed to a way of thinking about leadership that is collective and community-orientated. This means that they believe in a vision of leadership that allows everyone to own it, rather than it being something that only a particular group of individuals can achieve. Since social leaders want everyone to co-own leadership in ECEC, they take steps to make leadership something that feels like an everyday part of being an ECEC professional. They break down the mystique that can surround the term 'leadership' and share it as a concrete and achievable set of practices.

Case Study

Pauline Walmsley, CEO of Early Years

'If you set the table for development, people come to the table'

My role focuses on the effective recruitment and selection of people with ECEC expertise, creating the organization that allows people to grow – that makes them want to stay with us – and this is the basis of our succession planning. It's about building skills through mentoring and coaching. I can speak the language of the ECEC sector but I think the real professional expertise lies in the people we employ. My job is supporting them to grow and contribute.

When it comes to professional development, opportunities like the Erasmus programme have been absolutely brilliant. We've got a number of Erasmus programmes we're involved with. Really there's no financial benefit to us, but the non-financial benefit is that it gives our staff an opportunity to link internationally and to experience new opportunities and we can match some of the newer staff up with people who are more experienced. It helps them learn how to learn, and understand how to grow in their careers. It's less about the specifics of what they learn, it's more about understanding how to learn, how to grow, how to develop in your career. We try to invest time in that.

Money is always a struggle, particularly the investment needed to innovate and really improve practice with young children. I would love to be able to put people through a Master's Programme but financially we just cannot afford to do that at this point in time, and sadly, neither can I foresee a point in the future of being able to do that. So we have to keep an eye out to how best we can make opportunities for people. We're continually looking to Erasmus and other programmes to support professional development, and find projects to add value to another project in order to create some space for reflection. You're looking at how you can give staff certain experiences on a shoestring. It's a massive challenge.

If I had the money I think the possibilities are endless, I really do. I am a great believer in human curiosity and in human desire for growth and when that's nurtured it is transformational.

Developing leadership is fundamental to the sustainability of the sector since previous research shows that professionals in ECEC are often 'reluctant leaders'. They can be reticent about taking on the title of 'leader' and of engaging in formalized programmes of leadership development (Krieg et al., 2014). Social leaders have to reject this tendency and embed leadership development in the culture of the organization so that ECEC is a sector of strong, rather than reluctant, leaders. Brett Wigdortz, founder and CEO of Tiney, recognizes this dimension in the work that they do to build up leadership identity among home educators:

> *Working with small children is a leadership role. Sometimes I wonder if it's seen as less of a leadership role, because it's seen as a feminine role. It's certainly more of a leadership role than being an accountant. Accountants in the city are good at pretending to be leaders while early childhood educators shy away from being recognised as the leaders they clearly are!*

To support the wider identification with leadership across the ECEC sector, social leaders create organizations that consistently speak the language of leadership and embed it in daily practice. LEYF makes a point of building leadership development right from induction to influence how all staff see the value and importance of leadership in the organization. When someone joins LEYF, in whatever role, their first experience is an induction programme called 'Welcome to the Early Years'. Whether you're a finance assistant, HR officer, nursery manager, chef, area manager or apprentice everybody does this programme. It introduces you to the idea of a childcare social business, which is to deliver the best quality care and education no matter your role. When you complete the programme you have to ask yourself: 'What is my role in supporting the outcomes? What is my role in creating the best quality, accessible and inclusive education for young children?'. So right from day one the focus is on collectively leading social purpose.

Similarly, in the LEF in Toronto, the induction involves thinking about social enterprise and the purpose of LEF more broadly, as Peter Frampton explains:

> *We do a two day orientation for all staff called 'grow your own social enterprise' where we introduce LEF as a social enterprise. Even the kitchen staff do some basic decision-making and modelling around the social and economic aspects of social enterprise.*

In organizations committed to social leadership, the conversations about leadership do not stop at the induction. Leadership development scales and leadership programmes are built into the day-to-day work of the organization. Jacqueline Lamb uses dialogues about what leadership is in order to increase the sense of ownership among ECEC professionals. If professionals have defined what leadership is themselves, they can own it:

> *We've developed a handbook called 'What is leadership at Indigo?'. We developed it with the staff. We got a sample of staff from all different roles across the organisation and got them to talk about what they saw as being leadership and how that was delivered in the organisation and the kinds of things they saw in their role that demonstrated leadership.*

Bringing leadership to life means describing what it looks like, through examples, that are situated in the everyday work of individuals at all levels. Few books on leadership specifically talk about it in an ECEC context and explain, in practical terms for those who are not in formal leadership roles, that 'when you do this, it's leadership'. Even research aimed at highlighting core ECEC leadership practices (e.g. Cheung et al., 2019) tend to do this in abstract terms. What does it really mean when we say that a core leadership practice is 'designing curriculum delivery in relation to the school-based needs' (as identified in the research of Cheung et al.)? What does that look like? How does it feel? How does it play out in an everyday context of an apprentice or a room leader for example? Mandy Cuttler at LEYF explains how you can make leadership into something more concrete through noticing and naming leadership behaviours when they occur:

> *There's the person that runs away when there's a cranky parent at the door and the person who might be terrified but steps up. Who is showing some leadership there? Sometimes that needs to be reflected back to them. You might say you have shown some great leadership here, in that you stepped up, you were fearful, but you didn't shirk your leadership responsibilities, and you demonstrated that actually you could engage with this person. You need to be able to also describe what leadership looks like in action. People in ECEC are very visual and like a metaphor or a visual image to help them recognise the action they took was leadership in action.*

Social leaders in ECEC look for examples of leadership at all levels and document them, so that they can share these examples of leadership with others. They engage others in discussions about what leadership is and how it manifests day-to-day through everyday practice. Through this they support everyone in an organization, regardless of their formal role, to see the behaviours they engage in day-to-day that constitute leadership.

Drawing leadership out through action research

Social leaders help individuals to step up and develop their leadership capacities through processes such as coaching. As noted earlier in the chapter, many working in ECEC will not immediately identify themselves as a 'leader'. One way that social leaders draw individuals out of themselves and help them to recognize their own leadership potential is through action research. The process of action research creates a learning environment where staff are encouraged to constantly observe and think about what could be better, plan how these improvements might be achieved, and then monitor whether changes actually do constitute improvements, and how they need to be refined further. This cycle is the work of leadership in action. When professionals carry out action research, they are learning how to lead.

At LEYF, action research is a fundamental part of investing in leadership development across the organization. It is written into a strand of the pedagogy called Leadership for Excellence. According to Mandy Cuttler, Head of Pedagogy at LEYF, action research drives leadership by building professional confidence and reflection, as well as community and collaboration across the organization. Action research at LEYF has three simple phases, developed from the work of Stringer (1999):

- Look – gathering information to understand what is going on; defining the problem or question that needs more investigation and making sure you're clear on the context.
- Think – collecting evidence, interpreting what it means and what it suggests about the problem and its solution. Identifying an action to take and agreeing how to measure whether the action has been effective.
- Act – test whether the action resolves the problem or addresses the question. Evaluate and share the learning from the process. Devise next steps.

How these three phases are enacted is varied across the organization and is open to anyone whether an apprentice, a manager or someone working in the central office team for LEYF. An apprentice might be interested in, for example, the potential of woodwork to develop children's concentration or a manager may want to lead on drama or sustainability. They all have an opportunity to investigate this, working through the three stages with the potential to embed their findings across the organization as a means of ensuring continuous improvement. Managers are trained to support colleagues in developing action research projects.

It is not just at LEYF that action research works to build leadership. International research shows the same pattern. For example, Henderson (2017) evaluated the impact of action research on leadership development among ECEC professionals in an independent school context in Australia. Through in-depth interviews before and after their engagement with action research, Henderson found that the experience of action research greatly increased the professionals' sense of leadership and ownership through two types of process: relational work and identity work.

- Relational work. The action research worked to develop professionalism and capacity because it made time for reflection, connection and collaborative innovation among the group of teachers involved. The 'relational work' between teachers was effective because it was underpinned by a shared purpose and it had the time it needed to develop organically. If the same professionals had come together for a coffee morning once a week for example, they would not have developed the levels of interconnectedness and wholeness that emerged as a result of this action research experience. The teachers did often find it challenging to invest the time required, but when time was particularly limited, they used a more structured approach to frame the meetings such as listening protocols, which helped them to make intensive use of the time together.
- Identity work. The action research experience involved 'identity work' in that there was deep questioning and challenge. As discussed earlier in the chapter, collaborative innovation will involve disagreements and tensions – it is not always plain sailing. The professionals involved in this study found that their own identities as pedagogues changed over the course of the project. They questioned themselves about how they did things, as well as voicing their own ideas.

Overall, the experience of the action research led to increased levels of confidence among the professionals. They were more confident about sharing their own ideas, perspectives and experiences and using these as the basis for change, implemented through reflective cycles in collaborative learning groups. Social leadership makes use of this robust connection between action research and leadership development, using action research as a key way to foster leadership across an organization for every single professional.

Conclusion

Investing in others' leadership is a fundamental element of the social leadership model. Social leaders understand the importance of building and maintaining an organizational culture that prioritizes the leadership of others. They see that this is an important driver of quality, as well as supporting professionals to take more meaning from their work in ECEC. This shift has knock-on positive effects, including improvements in recruitment, retention and staff well-being, which in turn impacts positively on quality. It is a virtuous cycle. To support leadership to flourish in an organization, social leaders embed core practices including distributed leadership, coaching, JEPD and action research. They talk the language of leadership in a way that makes it accessible to all, showing through examples what leadership looks like on the ground and drawing everyone into discussions of leadership, including those who might not readily identify themselves as leaders.

5

Facilitating powerful conversations

This chapter considers the fifth element of social leadership: the facilitation of powerful conversations across ECEC. We address three questions:

1. Why do social leaders need to facilitate powerful conversations in ECEC?
2. What makes a conversation a 'powerful conversation'?
3. How are powerful conversations part of the everyday work of social leaders and how do they ensure that they happen?

Why does facilitating powerful conversations matter in ECEC?

In this part of the chapter, we consider why it is so important for social leaders to facilitate powerful conversations in ECEC. We present three reasons why social leaders need to focus energy on the facilitation of powerful conversations, both within their organizations and further afield.

1. Powerful conversations are a cornerstone of democratic participation. Through conversations, embedded in pedagogy and organizational culture, social leaders develop the willingness and capacity of both children and adults to contribute more fully to society.
2. Through powerful conversations, social leaders contribute to the quality of ECEC delivery indirectly, by developing, nourishing and sustaining an organizational culture positive for recruitment, retention, well-being and collaborative innovation.
3. Conversations are an essential part of building the profile of ECEC within society and strengthening a collective, global voice for ECEC that can improve conditions within a sector that is often marginalized and under-valued.

The reasons for the importance of facilitating powerful conversations in ECEC social leadership are explored more in the following sections.

Powerful conversations as the basis for democracy

Powerful conversations matter to social leaders because they are the basis for democracy. Social leadership in ECEC involves an explicit and fierce commitment to laying the foundations for democratic participation in society. The link between conversations and democracy is well-established in educational philosophy, and we can trace it back through to Freire's critical pedagogy and before this, to the link made between education and democracy by Dewey. In bell hooks' pedagogical vision (1994, 2003), which builds on Freire's critical pedagogy, conversations are an essential part of developing education as a practice of freedom. Most of hooks' writing on pedagogy relates to older learners studying at university, but the principles of a conversational, engaged pedagogy apply regardless of age. For hooks, it is through conversations in the learning space – deep, open and authentic conversations – that learners can develop their own voice and find meaningful connections between their everyday lives and their learning in the classroom. As individuals work out a way to express themselves in conversations, this ripples outwards, affecting how they contribute to society more broadly. In this way, education becomes a starting point for social action and a means for individuals and groups to practise resistance as well as participation. Social pedagogies that commit energy to developing powerful conversations, in both frequency and depth, are therefore the backbone of a strong culture of democratic participation.

Zaridah Abu Zarin, CEO of the Horizon Early Childhood Centre in Kuala Lumpur, Malaysia, explains how conversations are key for developing autonomy and voice among professionals, which in turn feed into wider democratic participation in society:

Autonomy is very important, especially in our society. I often find it's very difficult to get professionals here to share their ideas and opinions. In a team meeting, I'll try to start a discussion about how we can achieve something together and the majority of the time, when we go around the table, all we can hear is the sound of the crickets. It's very difficult to encourage the professionals to contribute their own voice. I think it goes back to constraints in our culture. When you are a child, you are not allowed to ask questions or be involved in conversation. So, then it is difficult for adult professionals to develop ideas and participate in a critical discussion.

Social leaders enact a pedagogy that revolves around conversations; it is a parallel pedagogy in that it guides both learning for children and learning among professionals. Conversations with children, where we genuinely want to know what they think and feel, are central to developing their sense of voice, self-expression and autonomy. At the same time, conversations with and among professionals are key for developing not just the same characteristics but for enabling a virtuous cycle where they can have their own personal conversations with children. Zarin describes the need for social leaders to model powerful conversations for professionals who may not have grown up with others respecting their voice.

> *I was passing by a class, and it was naptime. I saw a child upset. I could see his facial expression, and I could hear the teacher saying to the brother 'go and look after your little brother' and continuing on with her work. So, I approached that teacher and I asked her to come with me. Together we sat down next to the little boy who was upset and I said 'what's the matter – are you ok?'. It turned out that his parents were going through a divorce and he wanted to talk about it. I cuddled him afterwards and read him a story and he went for his nap. After that, the teacher cried. She had not thought to start a conversation with the boy or to find out about what was upsetting him. I find many teachers are unfortunately oblivious to the opportunities for conversations with children, but I can try to model that and over time, hopefully, we can change things.*

Social leaders therefore look for opportunities to start or develop powerful conversations since these are the key to social change and democratic participation. Powerful conversations with children and families form a central tenet of a social pedagogy but are also key to professionalism in the sector and the development of voice and resistance among an often under-valued workforce struggling to make themselves heard.

Conversations are the key to organizational culture

Social leaders invest in powerful conversations because these are at the heart of a strong organizational culture, which in turn matters for process quality in ECEC and therefore to children's outcomes. When Jacqueline Lamb joined Indigo Childcare Group in Glasgow, Scotland, as the new CEO, she used conversations as the means to turn over a 'new leaf' in the organizational culture of Indigo:

> *For the first three months that I was here, I spent a large proportion of my time speaking individually to every member of staff and just having conversations with*

them – exploring what they thought about the organisation, what their hopes and dreams were for the organisation. In these conversations I could share my hopes and aspirations as well. I could tell them 'I don't want us to be just another childcare provider. I want us to be outstanding.' After these individual conversations, we continued our conversations on a larger scale. So, for the first year and a half that I was here, it was very much about having conversations about leadership with people. What leadership meant to them. What it meant to me. What it should mean in the organisation. This has become the basis for everything I've tried to do at Indigo to improve our practice and ultimately what we can provide to children and families.

In a qualitative evaluation of an action research initiative to foster leadership among ECEC professionals in Australia, Henderson (2017) suggested that the most important element was actually making time and space for meaningful, reflective conversations between professionals. This 'relational work' between professionals supported individuals' and organizational development because it enabled continuous quality improvement. Henderson's research demonstrates the power of professional conversations as a means for improving the quality of processes within ECEC organizations, which ultimately impacts on the children and families served by the organization. This is further supported in the research by Arbour et al. (2016), which highlights how continuous quality improvement – made possible through regular professional conversations – was an essential part of improving the effectiveness of an intervention designed to improve process quality in Chilean ECEC. The researchers found that it was not enough to provide regular and intensive training for teachers through workshops. When structured conversations were added into this mix, significantly more progress was made by both individuals and the overarching organization.

Of course, it's not just about the number of conversations that you have but about the quality of these conversations. We all know that increased levels of communication can sometimes be detrimental to, rather than supportive of, relationships. Just think about the last time you experienced a flurry of emails within a team, with everyone copied into short back and forth exchanges between specific members. These experiences typically bring about feelings of disconnection and resentment. What matters for organizational culture then is not just the frequency of conversations but how these conversations look and feel. This is where the need for 'powerful conversations' matters. Powerful conversations are transformative. They are not a rapid volley backwards and forwards, but a more expansive dialogue in which we rethink and maybe change some aspect of our initial thought or behaviour. We tend to leave powerful conversations thinking about something differently, with a new idea or experiencing a connection or re-connection with ourselves or others. Chantal Williams, CEO of Stepping Stones in Tasmania, Australia, explains how these powerful conversations can actually emerge in gentle exchanges on the floor amidst the children:

> *The pedagogical leader doesn't take anyone away and say let's make a plan. She uses quiet, gentle conversations, gentle pushes, gentle suggestions and then helps with scaffolding where they [the professionals] want to be.*

LEYF have changed the language of supervision and appraisal by designing a system of professional performance conversations to support our talent enrichment approach. This has fostered more deep and powerful conversations. This has also led to much more equitable discussions which align with the research showing that when we minimize those hierarchical differences, there is a greater flourishing of what Meyerson (2008) calls 'positive deviance', whereby individuals come up with new and better ways of doing things that can then shape practices across the entire organization.

Powerful conversations are a part of the organizational culture that social leaders develop, nourish and sustain over time. Some organizations may make an explicit commitment to democracy, dialogue or connection, but without developing powerful conversations as an everyday aspect of their organizational culture. This is the case when we consider the research of Federico Farini (in press), looking at how pedagogical planning meetings operate in the context of Reggio Emilia ECEC settings. Farini's research demonstrates that a stated commitment to relational pedagogies with children does not necessarily translate into participatory and inclusive conversations between professionals working in the same setting. Through his intensive observations of team pedagogical planning meetings in two Reggio Emilia settings, and a particular focus on the conflicts that can emerge in these spaces, Farini found that professional conversations could unfold in different ways. He identified two main categories to describe these conversations: hierarchical management and participative management. Hierarchical management involved shutting down personal expressions in the pedagogical planning meeting through reference to roles (e.g. 'I am more senior than you') while participative management used conversations as a means to draw out the voice of all those present in the meeting and reach a collaborative consensus for moving forward in practice (e.g. 'you are the expert, so what do you think?').

The ECEC leadership team at the Learning Enrichment Foundation (LEF) in Toronto, Canada, expressed how highly participatory conversations were part of the everyday culture of the organization. Peter Frampton, CEO, explains:

> *It's messy. When we look at streamlining our operations, our a-ha moment was realising that in our most inefficient moments, we achieve most of our mission. Our client intake form can be done online in this or that way, but by keeping it offline we facilitate a conversation about a child and a family, and that really matters. As a social business, you're balancing that. You're saying that the mission is really around building relationships and everything has to flow from that. So 'inefficient' conversations are key to this.*

Katrina Estey, Director of School Age Children at LEF, explained how this also influences how they conduct professional conversations, giving the example of a recent recruitment decision.

> *We had some supervisor positions being confirmed and we had to agree who would be appointed and one of the candidates was an internal applicant. So how many conversations did we have? Something like five! We got senior managers together and said let's really talk about this. What does it look like for the organisation? What does it look like for that person moving into the role? What does it look like for that team? It would have been a lot easier for us to say 'no that's not right let's move her here', that's a lot easier. But five hours later, we reached a fuller, much richer conclusion. So that's where we're different from other organisations – through that truly collaborative conversation. Yes, lots of people say that they do it but it's engrained here. That's how you know someone is really part of the LEF team, because they ask the question and they want to talk about it before it's just an automatic decision. And that's how you recognise when people choose to leave, and that's ok too, because they're not really in that same headspace. That truly collaborative conversation is different and it takes a special energy.*

Making powerful conversations part of the organizational culture impacts on many variables that in turn influence the quality of ECEC provision. These include:

- Recruitment and retention. Professionals want to work in organizations that offer the potential for personal transformation (Jironet, 2020). Powerful conversations therefore engender a culture that many are drawn to. They will recommend the organization to friends as a place to work, and will remain with the organization (and sector) if they feel that their needs for 'identity work' and 'relational work' are met.

- Well-being and motivation. While the 'identity work' offered by powerful conversations can be tiring, it also offers a level of meaning and sense of purpose that is vital to professionals' well-being in the workplace (Robinson-Hickman & Sorenson, 2014). When people feel professionally well, they are willing to bring more of their whole selves to the work of the organization in order to support its flourishing (Guglielmo & Palsule, 2014). This is not just about giving more time to the organization (e.g. staying late) but rather about contributing innovations that support the development of the organization.

Powerful conversations to build voice across the ECEC sector

It is no secret that the ECEC sector around the world is fragmented. In most parts of the world, ECEC is delivered through a mixed economy model, with a mixture of state-funded, private, charitable or hybrid (e.g. social enterprise) settings. The sector is also predominantly financially precarious (particularly for smaller providers) and fragmented so that it is difficult to find a strong collective voice for the sector that cuts across different types of organizational context. Dearbhala Cox-Giffin, Director of Childcare at Giraffe Childcare in Dublin, Ireland, talks about the tensions that often exist between Government and the ECEC sector in Ireland:

An ECEC sector that is fit for purpose for children and their families is born from real and meaningful partnership between Government and the sector where long term plans and decisions which have implications for the delivery of a service are discussed and agreed together. Consultation and communication with the sector are critical to engage all partners to embed quality for our youngest children. The ECEC sector has evolved without a clear Government vision and has been greatly underfunded in Ireland. Thankfully this is slowly being addressed but it is still not enough and does not go far enough. The sector has to be on board to make the Government's vision a reality.

Although Cox-Giffin is describing the Irish context, it feels familiar to many ECEC colleagues in other parts of the world. Conversations offer a way forward, beyond the current fragmentation and lack of vision. It is only through powerful conversations that the sector can come together, not just on a national level but an international level too. Keya Lamba, founder of the international ECEC community 'Early Insights', explains the importance of establishing these global connections as a foundation for a strong ECEC voice in the future.

The ECEC field needs a global movement equivalent to the girls education movement or climate change to get it to the top of everyone's radar. This is what Early Insights hopes to do: inspire a global movement for early childhood by creating connections, exchanging knowledge and amplifying the voice of early education and care. ECEC is a field where having a global conversation is critical to build this movement. The global perspective is invaluable and this was made clear to our community during the pandemic. Early educators in the global north learned a lot from early educators in countries like Lebanon who had been through disrupted education and school closures before. Although the world's education systems are very diverse and each country has its unique issues, the early childhood age group has the most universal developmental milestones that can benefit from a global perspective. Our global community of early childhood educators has found we have more in common than we have apart and there is real power in learning from one another in our different countries.

What is a powerful conversation?

In this part of the chapter, we explore what turns an ordinary conversation into a powerful conversation. We present three characteristics of powerful conversations. These are:

1. Trust
2. Empathy
3. Bravery

Each of these characteristics is explained, using quotes from ECEC social leaders from around the world to bring them to life and show how they look and feel on the ground.

Trust

In 2009, when Anthony Seldon was Headmaster of Marlborough College, he was concerned about the future his students faced especially in what he identified was a reduction in trust. He thought that this lack of trust was spurred on by the easy mobility of modern life and the pace of technological change, both of which reduced the time available for trusting relationships to develop. He described a trust filled childhood as:

belonging to a trustworthy family and living in a trusting neighbourhood are a crucial grounding for a life which would be happy and worthwhile. To enjoy these benefits requires neither wealth nor privilege yet will confer advantages that money can never buy. Those experiencing a childhood not characterised by trusting relations, will experience a community which is atomised and will be more likely to lead a life full of suspicion and anxiety.

(Seldon, 2009, p. 175)

Social leaders must find ways to promote trust on the ground and one way is to ensure people have an equal voice in developing new ways of operating. They feel more assured that their concerns will be addressed and that changes can work to their advantage. However, when their trust and a sense of common good is lacking it can generate widespread anger, fear and resentment leading to bigotry and political upheaval. Alice Sharp, CEO of Experiential Play in Glasgow, Scotland, explains how important trust is in the context of her organization and for forging relationships between professionals within the organization:

Trust is one of our core values. That means every one of my staff are completely utterly reliable and trustworthy. We develop that trust between ourselves and with everyone we support. I know that confidentiality doesn't even have to be mentioned because it's just kept. I know as well that staff will know if there's a crisis with one of the candidates, for instance one of the students couldn't afford to buy food and so we worked out a system. When she came in and hadn't had breakfast she would indicate to one of the staff team, who would then go and hide a food pack in the bathroom. That way, she wouldn't have to ask for it and it wouldn't be embarrassing.

According to Reich (2019) to ensure we support the common good we need leadership that puts trust at its centre. He thinks that one element of a leaders' role is to uphold and strengthen the institution they govern to rebuild public trust. He describes leadership as a noble cause defined not by personal ambition but by morality and purpose. Reich (2019) also noted the importance of trust particularly in the days of digital social media where people continue to challenge the veracity of information and intention. He notes how leaders need to consider their role in building civic trust which he believes is both self-enforcing and self-perpetuating but also necessary to cope with the fear of the disruptions that are caused by new ideas and new technology.

Osinga (2007) notes that for individual and organizations to thrive in uncertainty we need agility and leadership that builds trust because that will encourage cooperation and space for creativity and innovation. Dan Wise a Senior Director at LEF in Canada talked about 'moving at the speed of trust'.

He was referencing the Covid response in the organization especially from their leader Peter Frampton and the need to encourage trust.

> *a couple of weeks into the pandemic lockdown, we started to really understand the impact of Covid and then Peter [the CEO of Learning Enrichment Foundation] started talking about moving at the speed of trust. Because people, including ourselves, were freaking out a little bit. In the early days things were literally changing by the hour. Where the Government would say ok do this and we would make our changes, and then the Government would say oh wait a second hang on we're going to do this instead. The result was people lost trust in their elected officials, even though they were the ones with the microphones that could access the public. Instead, parents and staff looked to us to respond appropriately and consistently but without overwhelming them.*

Building trust requires leaders to be open and authentic through consistent unbiased action which displays empathy. Organizations led by social leaders who build trust demonstrate ten characteristics described by Seldon (2009) and which we have summarized as:

1. ethical values
2. organizations which exhibit pride and a sense of ownership
3. organizations with responsibilities and duties rather than just rights
4. responsibilities are more than the mere maximization of profit and personal gain
5. regimes which guarantee freedom from fear
6. ably and wisely led
7. honest communication
8. those within the organization are looked after and have rights guaranteed
9. the family is respected and supported
10. there is human scale: individuals feel known and valued

Empathy

Building trust has even more significance in the light of Garnett's (2018) observation that empathy appears to be on the wane causing what is now known as empathy deficit. Empathy is the ability to walk in someone's shoes and act in a way that is sensitive to other people's perspectives. Garnett (2018) refers to studies in the United States among college students which identified a 48 per cent drop in cognitive and affective empathy. This describes peoples' ability to understand how someone else is feeling and respond to their pain and distress.

Instead of empathy there was a significant rise in narcissism. The studies could not link this to one specific reason but noted that social media and the rise in digital gaming were not helping.

But while there is evidence of a decline in empathy, there is a paradoxical rise in people's interest in the subject with Internet searches for 'empathy' doubling as more people begin to consider empathy and our compassion for people of all over the world as one of the building blocks to World Peace.

For those working in ECEC this is unsurprising as empathy is considered an essential step in supporting children to be kind and considerate, building pro social behaviour, social and communication skills. Garnett recommends that empathy needs to be developed as part of the pedagogy so that we can nurture and sustain compassionate and tolerant communities of parents, staff and children. The social leader recognizes the importance of trust and empathy as central to how we balance the benefits and challenges of the digital age. One key route to doing this is through the power of conversations. The social leader uses conversations as the means to develop and support a trusting culture.

Conversation is often considered the active interaction between two people and dialogue is broader in that it will also describe written conversations such as on email or online. The social leader uses the term conversation in its broadest sense and the conversation can operate orally, online or via written email correspondence. We don't often expect everyday conversations to be thoughtful or reflective but simply to translate information. However, social leaders understand the power of conversations and the context in which they are framed and delivered. Conversation is an opportunity to inform, request or persuade in a way that leaves both parties better informed. Conversation is purposeful and goal directed and is rarely an end in itself. Conversation is a social relationship involving people working together with a chance for everyone to participate. Openness to the possible truth of what the other is saying is also required. This has an 'emotional' side. Conversation involves:

- **Concern**. To be with people, engaging them in conversation involves a commitment to each other. We feel something for the other person as well as the topic.
- **Trust**. We have to take what others are saying in good faith. This is not the same as being gullible. While we may take things on trust, we will be looking to check whether our trust is being abused.
- **Respect**. While there may be large differences between partners in conversation, the process can only go on if there is mutual regard.

- **Appreciation**. Linked to respect, this involves valuing the unique qualities that others bring.
- **Affection**. Conversation involves a feeling with, and for, those taking part.
- **Hope**. We engage in conversation in the belief that it holds possibility. Often it is not clear what we will gain or learn, but faith in the process carries us forward.

Eliana Elias, US coach in ECEC, describes a new vision of leadership that places an 'ethics of care' at its centre:

> *Care is something that is so connected to women that ethics of care has been de-valued historically, so I think there is a huge connection between sexism and the way early childhood has been promoted or funded. And now that we have these amazing national, international women leaders and we are seeing what's happening with New Zealand, what's happening in Germany, what's happening in Denmark, and I have a feeling that this ethics of care, which is primarily championed by women leaders, is going to become more legitimate. So I think there is this huge connection here about this notion of how we legitimize leadership that is empathic, strong, but also consider feelings so we end up marrying the heart and the mind. This challenges the misconception that if you think with your heart, you can't make rational decisions but now it's time to really marry the two, and legitimize this ethics of care.*

Of course, empathy is about far more than just what we say. It is demonstrated physically, through our body language, facial expression and touch. One way to think about empathy is as an empathic response chain (Bertrand et al., 2018). Within this chain, physical mimicry of another person is the first step in building an empathic response. When we begin to feel and show empathy, we will readily mimic the facial expression or body posture of the person we are empathizing with. Touch is another way to establish an empathic connection and social leaders may instinctively use touch as a way to foster empathy within organizations. Dearbhala Cox-Giffin, Director of Childcare at Giraffe Childcare in Ireland, explains the challenges brought about the Covid-19 pandemic in terms of demonstrating empathy with others through close physical connection and relaxed moments of touch:

> *You know when someone tells you something funny, and you put your hand on them, it's that whole physical thing. If you don't have that anymore, it completely changes how you interact with others. That care and warmth and affection is part of our sector. It's what we do with children and it's what we do with each other. I think this leadership style is quite sector specific. I think it would be similar in care homes, hospitals – it's a different kind of business when people are your everyday.*

Bravery

Showing empathy and care is not just about 'being nice'. It has the power to shift organizational culture from transaction to transformation. Empathy is a foundation for openness and honesty, which in turn enables greater development and learning. Kim Scott (2017) describes how, when leaders are brave, they can embody 'radical candour', helping others to see where and how their practice needs to improve. When leaders develop their capacity to enact radical candour, they can influence greater change and development. Honest feedback without a grounding of authentic care is more likely to be rejected by those receiving it, but when we believe that the person giving us feedback deeply cares about us and our future, we are more likely to hear and respond to the feedback positively. The key here is psychological safety. In twenty years of research analysing all different kinds of team in action in the workplace, Amy Edmondson (2018) found that the element in teams that made the biggest difference to whether they were effective or not was psychological safety. In the teams where people felt that they – as their whole selves – were emotionally held and cared for by others, individuals were more likely to genuinely reflect, to make change where it was needed, to correct each other and to innovate. This is echoed in Brene Brown's work around the power of vulnerability for enabling development and change at an individual and organizational level. When we open ourselves up, we are in a position to grow and learn, and opening ourselves up is more likely to happen in situations where we experience and extend authentic care.

It is essential to recognize that learning is part of an empathic response and truly empathic conversations in ECEC will involve challenge and the push to move forward together. It is not just that an ethics of care lays the groundwork for developing others. Developing others, through careful and continuous feedback, is part of feeling and showing empathy. To put it another way, just meeting people where they are at and holding them there, without initiating any movement or progress, is not a demonstration of authentic care. Californian ECE coaches Barbra Blender and Eliana Elias talk about this with passion in relation to the teachers and the leaders that they coach:

> *Eliana: I think the downfall of a lot of our leaders in early childhood is that we stay too much in the emotional space, in the caring. 'Oh yeah, they are going through so much stress, I understand, I acknowledge'. But we don't push enough. We don't ask: 'so what are we going to do about it?'. I sound harsh. But I feel that there needs to be a balance. I'm willing to listen and to be empathic but every coaching meeting I do, ends with 'ok what are we going to do about it?'. Because I don't want to live just in*

that space of 'I acknowledge, it's hard, you're stressed, give you a hug' but I want to say 'yeah, it's hard, let's move on what are we going to do about it?'. It's important to be able to attune with the emotional state of the teachers and the leaders, but don't stay there, don't get sucked in to that emotional state.

Barbra: *If you do [get sucked in to that emotional state], it's eventually disempowering for the person you're coaching. It's what takes away everyone's power or their perception of power. When we just stay there, it's patronising quite frankly, to not assume that who you're working with wants more, has ideas. We need to flip the script so that they're not subject to whatever happens, and they get to write the ending of that chapter.*

Social leaders do not 'just' empathize through conversations with professionals or parents, they use these conversations as a place to offer productive challenge. The conversations are an opportunity to 'flip the script' and set up possibilities for living, thinking, being and doing differently within ECEC. Empathy is a foundation for these new possibilities, but it also requires the willingness to be brave and take risks in the challenges that you offer through conversations. Cecil Beaton (1904–80) is credited with saying:

Be daring, be different, be impractical, be anything that will assert integrity of purpose and imaginative vision against the play it safers, the creatures of the commonplace, the slaves of the ordinary.

Social leaders in ECEC pay attention to Beaton's focus on us being daring and different but always link it to the integrity of our vision. Conversations offer a forum in which to be different and daring, to be bold and try to move forward with solutions. This is good advice to all leaders of ECEC as we are preparing children for a life we can neither imagine nor describe. ECEC leaders must understand that change is a central element of leadership as change is not just driven by external factors such as the digital social age. It is also driven by the internal changes led by new children, new learning, new resources and the action research that is so important to the continual cycle of improvement necessary for any service wanting to provide a high-quality pedagogy for both staff and children.

Across the wider ECEC sector, leaders must address the abilities of settings to create a culture which allows both the children and the staff to take risks with their own learning and development in an atmosphere of empowerment and ultimately in a way that can lead to acts of activism and advocacy. This starts with brave conversations. For example, conversations can be the fertile ground in which staff voice new ideas and introduce topics that could be controversial.

For example, at London Early Years Foundation (LEYF) we introduced Drag Queen Story Time to use the fun theatricality of Drag Queens telling stories as one way to challenge some children's increasing reliance on the screen as the storyteller. It also provided a space to open up wider conversations with children and parents as a way of building empathy and kindness when dealing with the diverse and the unusual. For others, taking a risk may be more structural such as raising issues of social justice and fairness and advocating for the rights of all children to access nurseries. Leaders need to be clear how this is discussed across the organization balancing the benefits of social media to create a digital conversation but also recognizing the limitations of these discussions becoming a game of ping pong rather than a deep philosophical conversation.

To facilitate deeper conversations, Peter Frampton and his team at the LEF in Canada try and embed research into their structures.

> *We don't have a research department but building a positive attitude to research drives academic rigour and this means staff are motivated to engage and explore practice and ideas which keeps them motivated and makes them proud of what they do so it helps keep their eye on the ball.*

How do social leaders enact powerful conversations?

In the final part of this chapter, we consider how social leaders use four types of powerful conversation as part of their everyday practice. These conversations are the basis for all the other elements in the social leadership model. Pedagogical conversations are an integral part of driving a social pedagogy. Coaching conversations are essential to investing in and develop others' leadership. Network conversations and wider public conversations grow a shared sense of social purpose that can then become more effectively the driving force in ECEC, overcoming the fragmentation of the sector and enabling a stronger, more authoritative global ECEC voice to emerge. We consider each of these types of conversation in more depth below.

Pedagogical conversations

Powerful conversations are essential for building the trust and connection with parents and families that is needed in order to have a genuine impact through ECEC. Let's begin with the pedagogical conversation between the staff and parents. These are conversations designed to lead to pedagogical learning by helping both parties come to a greater understanding which leads to the ability to stop and reflect.

Every situation in an ECEC setting can be a catalyst for a pedagogical conversation, beginning with planned and formalized opportunities on day one when the key person meets new parents, leads a show around and completes the settling in procedure. This relationship is deepened through routine conversations as the child settles into the setting and the conversations become regular with routine chats at arrival and departure times, and then the more specific planned conversations about the child's progress, weekly planning checks to ascertain the child's interests at home, the completion of learning journeys and parents' evenings, workshops and events.

At LEYF two words are essential in any pedagogical conversation and that is *because* and *so*. These two words help to construct knowledge and supports thinking in a way that builds trust. Regular conversations at 'pick up' times might begin with 'Claude had a great day today, he really showed us his interest in cars. Maybe when you're walking home, you could ask him to point out his favourite cars on the walk home, saying what colour they are. This would be great because we are learning about colours at the moment so using Claude's interest in cars to introduce colours is a great teaching tool.'

A similar conversation between two staff opens up more learning for example when asking 'why did you design this display using such theory quotes?' A professional might respond 'Because I wanted it to be a teaching tool for parents so they could see evidence of language learning through the photos linked to the pedagogy theory quotes and our pedagogy. I thought the formality would give credibility to the message.'

Using conversations which reflect the relationship with parents helps build a more mutually trustful relationship for parents to be willing to fully engage. For example, admitting that their child can be uncooperative and very trying especially in the morning is difficult in the age of social media which bombard parents with images of the perfect parental relationship. To admit that their daughter can be awkward is for some parents a sign of parental failure. To be able to hold a warm and empathetic conversation with the staff member is essential; not just sharing the information but also as an opportunity for learning.

Experienced ECEC staff learn to spot the signs of when someone is ready to engage. They sense a situation or pick up a vibe from a parent that they are in the mood to talk and these conversations can unpick complex issues far more humanely and effectively. The social leader embeds a culture of sensitivity through the use of conversations and by doing so gives a voice to the staff encouraging them to articulate, explain and defend their position with regards to their actions, engagement, communication, decisions and pedagogical position. The resulting conversations are more effective because they are framed within a culture where staff have learned the art of conversing to clarify ideas, solve problems or reflect and consider a situation. It is the best use of a most natural activity. At LEYF training in oracy is considered essential whether you are an apprentice or a manager, a chef or a customer service officer. Nichole Leigh Mosty comments on her experience of driving pedagogical change in the United States and Iceland and noted the power of collaborative conversations to build a responsive social pedagogy that enables everyone to progress. This is considered in more detail as part of the case study below.

Case Study

Collaborative pedagogical conversations in Ösp Playschool

Nichole Leigh Mosty, former Director of Ösp Playschool

Pedagogical conversations are a key part of reflecting the values that are integral to Ösp Playschool, but also to me as an individual. Two of the most important values when we are thinking about pedagogical conversations are:

Appreciate and support the bond between child and family. That's something I've been able to carry over into the community development work that I do now. Because now I'm not working in the early childhood setting, I work in different projects where I'm using support system for parents. I'm working on a huge project right now where we're trying to involve parents much more in children's sport and leisure activities as a manner of connecting them socially to other children, and strengthening the bonds and ties to Icelandic learning.

Recognize that children are best understood and supported in the context of family, culture, community and society. Because these are the things that will always be there – this is Bronfenbrenner at its core. We have to understand that children are right there at the centre of it all. It is a lifelong investment that goes both ways. When children are older they can invest right back into their community and their families. So, that cycle matters.

When we really pay attention to these values and attempt to live them truly, then we see that pedagogical conversations must also involve the parents and family of the child. It is only when we engage the whole family that we can turn pedagogical conversations into something that truly transforms the entire community.

So when I was working with Ösp, we decided to do a huge empowerment project where we taught Icelandic for parents. And it ended up being such a wonderful experience because through these collaborative learning activities we were able to support our bilingual children. What we did was extend our school day and offer Icelandic courses for the parents. The bilingual children were allowed an extended day in the school where we had our staff supporting the learning of Icelandic using new techniques to support mother tongue languages. We used lots of games for learning Icelandic, rather than sitting over them with the language instruction book. At the same time, we had this huge literacy push. We were told we need to have everyone as high functioning Icelandic speakers, even when you have children that speak five languages in the house. So, we were coming up with new ways through play and engagement with these bilingual children in one room, while parents were learning Icelandic through fun and engaging methods in another room. And this collaborative learning connected the families. They began doing things like learning to make Icelandic pancakes and setting up a role play restaurant with the children who invited the parents to their restaurant which meant reading the menu and playing restaurant with the children.

So that's maybe one of the things that happens when you prioritize these pedagogical conversations and pedagogical collaborations that ripple through the whole community – you have to be prepared to step back as the leader and allow things to develop organically.

Coaching conversations

Coaching is a powerful way to encourage and support staff to develop, deepen and apply their skills and knowledge with greater competence and assurance. There are a variety of coaching definitions, but the definition that best sums up our approach to coaching is by Executive Coach Ed Batista who defines coaching as 'asking questions that help people discover the answers that are right for them'. Well coached and supported staff perform more confidently and therefore achieve better results across every level of the organization. Coaching is a supportive rather than a directive approach that relies on the power of the coaching conversation; which opens up thinking and ideas and helps staff find a solution to many of their own questions. Coaching conversations contribute to an ongoing learning process where the leaders, managers and colleagues enable team members to build mastery – it's not a quick fix approach but it is a great way to help ECEC staff become pedagogically sound and master the art, craft and science of their ECEC pedagogy.

Social leaders choose a method of coaching that is self-sustaining and easy to embed so that staff use coaching to build trusting relationships with each other and in a way that also supports them to become more confident and competent. In ECEC settings leaders and managers are often considered to be the expert and therefore expected to offer all the answers and solutions to any situation. However, the coaching conversation eases this rather hefty expectation and instead of telling or suggesting the solution, the coaching conversation is much less directive and instead leads the staff member to solving the issue or finding the solution in a much more effective but indirective way. As Candice Frankovelgia of the Center for Creative Leadership says, 'If you keep providing all the answers, people will keep lining up at your door looking for them.'

At the LEF, the senior team became aware of a deep organizational cultural shift that occurred when they placed a greater emphasis on coaching conversations where the standard response to questions was simply: 'well what do you think?' Using this refrain emphasizes the agency of the person asking the question. It gives them the opportunity and the permission to look inside themselves and build their own reasoning capacities and their own relevant experience. Katrina Estey, Director of School Age Children at LEF, explains just how much this can shape the culture within the organization:

> *When I started at LEF, supervisors would wait for decisions to come from Head Office. They really held back, waiting to be told, and so I would go to their meeting and ask them – 'what do you think? What's your decision?' – They were anxious, unused to giving their opinions and would try and get me to tell them the answers because that is what they were used to and it had filtered down to the educators too. Once we started to encourage the coaching conversations it really helped to engrain that as part of their leadership. So now, when you get a question from a supervisor and you say 'what do you think?' they say 'I knew you were going to say that!'*

Social leaders must provide a safe, nurturing and creative environment where every staff member learns to use the coaching conversation to express their ideas and find their own route to improve their practice and deepen their knowledge and understanding. While many coaching conversations are informal and the result of a sensitive leader noting the opportunity to explore an idea or bolster a relationship, in the same way as teachers and practitioners do with parents, other conversations are more formal and are designed around performance improvement or resolving an issue of conflict. How feedback is built into the conversation is key to the success of the engagement, leaving both parties clear and positive about their next set of actions, goals and successes even if it is to have another conversation soon.

Case Study

Eliana Elias, ECEC Coach based in California, US

Making thinking visible through coaching

One of the things that I've adopted as part of my practice is to really develop a parallel pedagogy between the things we want the teachers to be doing with the children and the things I do with the teachers. So say we believe that children should have autonomy over their learning process and choice. I try in my coaching to give that opportunity to the teachers as well, for example – I was working with a teacher who is an immigrant from China who is very very shy and quiet, but a very deep thinker. And her teaching community didn't see how deep of a thinker she was because she spoke English with difficulty, and yet her documentation was amazing. So I supported her in making her thinking visible by making her documentation shine through, and it ended up that we even produced a little article that got published, so she got a lot of visibility and now she has a lot more autonomy and recognition. So that's one tiny example.

The other one was something that Barbra came up with that is now getting a lot of traction. We've been doing these articles called '*Teaching behind the mask*' where we basically interviewed two teachers, and shaped their interview as a story, because we find that stories are quite powerful in highlighting social justice issues. We can read all we want about data and statistics but it doesn't register until you bring it alive with a real example. We told the stories of these real people who are so committed. We got them published in a fantastic local online publication called 48 Hills, and now we really want to make use of them in other circles as well. So those are two tiny examples of our stance.

There is a book that I really love called 'From Teaching to Thinking' which is written by Margie Carter and Ann Pelo and it lays out this roadmap about how to support teacher thinking, rather than telling them what to do. And that I think is a good descriptor of how Barbra and I approach our coaching, not with small tasks and skills, but with concepts that the teachers can apply in different ways. So, they can still be who they are – and of course, there are moments when we give them skills, we say 'no let's move this here' but most of our approach, is – building a connection, building something from the inside out. And in that book, I wrote a little chapter for that book, called 'teachers as cultural workers' where I give another example of approaching coaching with empathy. I tell this story of a teacher who was left with two subs, she was inexperienced, and she started just yelling at the kids and she wasn't going to let them go outside if they didn't sit 'criss cross apple sauce.' And how I dealt with the coaching after that, from the lens of 'I'm not going to punish this teacher', I'm going to try and get to the bottom of her stress, and think about together how we're going to mend her relationships with the kids. So those are examples.

Network conversations

One way social leaders can manage the change driven by the digital social age is to build interconnected networks and share the challenge. Within the networks we need leaders who will encourage conversations. Social media can help this process. Outside of the ECEC world we are watching the rise of global networked communities. Driven by passion and purpose, groups of people from around the world are linking together in communities that are dramatically transforming the way we communicate, make choices, take decisions and engage with one another. These global communities are also sharing information and becoming points of influence in novel ways. Weick (1995) suggests that making sense of a mess requires making connections and formulating the problems together. This would be described by Putnam (2000) as social capital which is how he describes the means of building trust through networks, friendships, connections from across the globe. By making connections with one another, people build networks, share common values, build trust and create a sense of identity which often leads them to engage in wider civic duties and volunteering. The benefits of networks far out-weigh just the power of the relationships according to Putnam who suggests that the collective skills, knowledge, experience, facilities and organizations ensure greater returns in the quality of life for all but especially children. He argues that social capital is second only to poverty in the breadth and depth of its positive effect on children's lives. According to him:

> *child development is powerfully shaped by social capital ... trust, networks and norms of reciprocity within a child's family, school, peer groups and larger community have wide ranging effects on the child's opportunities and choices and, hence behaviour and development.*

(Putnam, 2000, p. 296)

Syed (2019) reminds us of the benefit of bringing together a network of diverse views, experiences and knowledge to problematize and make sense of the model which Smallbone et al. (2001) described as having the *potential* to generate an innovative synthesis. Networks offer the opportunity to build constant and constructive dialogue and help people to come together with like-minded people, share ideas and concerns and develop a united voice. Networks, in providing opportunities for people to connect and collaborate, also enable the creation of learning communities with a focus on enquiry and improvement building.

However, as we have already noted, social media is paradoxical in how it can be both positive and unhelpful. Smith and Lewis (2011) suggest that learning paradoxes arise through change and tensions between the old and new – 'a struggle between the comfort of the past and the uncertainty of the future' (Lewis, 2000, p. 766). Leaders need to be alert to this because when creating a community of interest it can be hard to manage the cacophony of voices on a digital platform despite the initial positive intentions to bring people together who appear to share ideas, interests and values. Non-digital communities are often more organic based on loose or ad hoc connections of place, friendship or activities (Brint, 2001) which shape their own narrative and personal relationships. What leaders need to achieve is a level of solidarity as the outcome of belonging when the group has a set of common goals.

Leaders need to recognize their role in ensuring the network is framed through positive and harmonious relationships, nourished on trust, empathy and openness. The benefits of social networks are the rich and democratic opportunities to share your voice and hear those of others who you might never have met or considered meeting. But networks will only work best when sharing learning from a trustful perspective and where people feel safe to disseminate information, reflect, share ideas and learn together. It is often the place where people innovate and take risks and consider new ways of doing things. A place for collaboration and innovation that can engage entire communities where leaders can create an upward spiral of communication leading people into broader and more open thinking, reflection and behaviour rather than the more closed down responses from the narrow downward spiral. This process is described as social translucence because it makes participants and their activities visible to one another and by doing this reshapes what we understand as transparency and openness.

Pauline Walmsley who leads the Northern Irish Early Years organization comments on the impact of social media and how it can be used to extend their network. This includes celebrating examples of members' work or highlighting things a member has done or achieved. She sees this as a way of leading by sharing stories and comments that

> *it helps others see the benefit of sharing their leadership especially when social media can lead to fabulous conversations across the globe without having to get on a plane. Covid has forced us to conquer our anxieties about how we use digital communication technologies and has helped us make a giant leap forward in our mastery of the technologies that enable us to communicate including developing a set of etiquette around how we use it. I am hopeful that this will continue and really impact on connections in the future.*

Wider public conversations

To influence an audience about your cause, it is important to begin conversations that involve hearts and minds, share emotions and bring it alive through an inspirational story. Emotions are contagious, and we pick up cues and nuances without ever realizing. How you feel matters more especially when presenting to staff, emotions over-ride intellect and if you want to influence people you need to appeal to their emotions and be able to read the audience so as to build empathy and rapport.

In the case study profiling Eliana Elias's approach to coaching ECEC professionals, she talks about re-framing conversations as stories. Conversations and networks provide stories and people respond very positively to stories and storytelling. According to Schank (1999), our human memory is story-based in that we use stories to catalogue, store, relive, repeat and retrieve information. The best way to persuade someone is by telling a compelling story because it arouses deep emotional responses in the listener which also helps to make it memorable.

Framing a story will make it even more powerful because once it is set within an organizing frame it will define the issue, explain who is responsible and indicate potential solutions. All of these are best conveyed through metaphorical language, images, stereotypes and anecdotes. Metaphorical language turns complex information into a brain friendly format so we can map our knowledge from something we have already experienced onto something that is new or different thus helping us relate emotionally to the story. It is the language of emotional persuasion but can be used negatively also so leaders need to operate within the lens of trust and openness when framing stories especially if they are using this means to present complex messages. For example, some of the issues within ECEC are deeply contested and the attempts by experts to share concerns in a fair and balanced about issues such as schoolification, baseline assessment and transition can be hard to present in a way that the issues are visible and clear to the public.

Jerome Bruner's seminal research in cognitive science illuminated the importance of stories for how we think about the world and how we bring structure to our experiences. In 'Acts of Meaning' (1990) and 'Making Stories: Law, Literature, Life' (2002), Bruner argues that stories are what make us human and they are the key to understanding human thinking, learning and connection. Stories are how we make meaning in our lives. This is more dramatically articulated by Will Storr in his investigation into the science of storytelling:

> *Humans might be in unique possession of the knowledge that our existence is essentially meaningless, but we carry on as if in ignorance of it. We beetle away happily, into our minutes, hours and days, with the fact of the void hovering over us ... The cure for the horror is story. Our brains distract us from this terrible truth by filling our lives with hopeful goals and encouraging us to strive for them. What we want, and the ups and downs of our struggle to get it, is the story of us all.*
>
> (Storr, 2019, p. 1)

Those working in marketing have seized on the importance of stories for connecting with people in a world that is cluttered with information. For example, Tasgal (2015) suggests that the key to communication for any organization is to recognize the need to prioritize meaning over information. In a world of constant information, we can overestimate its importance and its potential to influence others. Tasgal argues that in reality, individuals are rarely persuaded by information. Instead, it is stories that help us to shift into the headspace of generating ideas. Information therefore needs to be made meaningful through the framework of stories. Stories help us then to take on board new ideas as

Zarina Zarin of the Horizon Centre of Excellence in Kuala Lumpur, Malaysia explains:

> *My mother-in-law is 93 years old and she is very good at storytelling. Stories are how normally she would educate us. When she wants to remind us of something, or to guide us, she uses storytelling.*

We can see this power in the example of a LEYF nursery manager feeling inspired by hearing (via email) the story of a particular child from another nursery manager. Embedded within the story was the social purpose of the organization – the commitment to transforming the world one child at a time. The story in the email facilitated an emotional re-connection with this purpose of the organization.

As well as helping us to reconnect with our sense of purpose, stories also help us to connect emotionally with others around us. They can be supportive of good relationships at work, which are in turn essential for peaceful and harmonious ECEC settings. Nichole Leigh Mosty, former director of Ösp Playschool in Reykjavik, Iceland, described how sharing stories is a key way to find a connection to even the most apparently difficult members of a team. The stories present a foundation for the personal and professional development involved in a culture of continuous quality improvement:

> *[speaking about a team member Nichole had found it difficult to work with] I sat down and we shared my experiences and we found that common þráða (an Icelandic word pronounced thraw-tha, meaning 'thread') that we could gather around. It was that love for early childhood and the need for self-development. And we've built a relationship and now, to this day, it's amazing to see her, she's just moving up in the organisation and I can't wait to see her when she's a director.*

Stories also enable us to reconnect with ourselves, with our own values and vision for ECEC. When we are met with an abstract list of organizational values, we may not know whether or not they resonate. But through stories – by making the abstract personal and concrete – we can begin to reflect on whether these values connect with our own, and if so, how. A LEYF baby room leader explained a simple way of enabling this re-connection at the beginning of room team meetings. She would choose one of the four LEYF values (inspiring, brave, nurturing and fun) and ask everyone to reflect on a time when they recently showed that value in action. The examples could be big or small, personal or professional. Such stories, thought up in the moment, bring a new level of understanding of the organization, of others and of ourselves.

Stories enable you to connect with the outside world as well. They help you to change the perception of early childhood education, which is key to the advocacy work involved in social leadership. Alice Sharp, CEO of Experiential Play in Glasgow, Scotland, described how essential she felt stories were in helping others to understand the lives of children and families living in poverty and the unquestionable importance of ECEC in reaching out to them:

> *My whole business is built on telling stories. The stories of children and families, dads and mums that don't have a voice, stories give them a voice. I use their stories all the time without naming them. That real life story is vibrantly important to letting our sector understand poverty and low level academic understanding of life. The sector on a whole is quite middle class. I would love the politicians to walk in the shoes of some of our families.*

For Zarita, Zaridah, Zarimah and Zarinna Zarin, four sisters leading ECEC in Kuala Lumpur, Malaysia, the story that they use to frame their advocacy and community organizing work in ECEC is even more personal:

> *To cut a long story short, we had to grow up and fend for ourselves without parents, and without any adult guidance. It was a blessing in disguise. It made us stronger and wiser. We learned to be independent, but with that comes the push and inspiration to bring more understanding to other people about early education and how it can impact a person's life, how it can shape the person that you turn out to be.*

Stories enable connection within the organization, but they also create the capacity for organizations to connect with those outside of the organization. They are a means for influencing how others see you and the children and the families that you serve. Social leaders use storytelling as a way to connect, to persuade and to inform. They engage with the power of stories for creating a culture of connection.

Conclusion

In this chapter we have considered why social leaders need to facilitate powerful conversations, what makes a conversation a powerful one, and how exactly social leaders start and sustain powerful conversations. More powerful conversations are urgently needed in ECEC because they are key to the democratic force of ECEC, the organizational culture that we seek to create and the need to build a stronger global voice for the sector to raise the profile and purpose of the sector. Powerful conversations are based on the principles of trust, empathy, challenge and risk-taking. Social leaders use these kinds of conversations to fulfil the other elements of the social leadership model. Pedagogical conversations are integral to driving a social pedagogy; coaching conversations enable a culture of leadership to flourish across organizations and the sector more broadly; network and public conversations are needed to build a stronger sense of voice across an often fragmented sector, and to ensure that we can effectively tell the story of ECEC to those who can support its future. The call to action embedded in this chapter is to start and sustain more powerful conversations. It means continuously developing your capacity to carry out powerful conversations – an ability that is always growing and never static – but also your bravery to start and develop the conversations that really matter and have the potential to shape the future of ECEC.

6

Sowing the seeds of sustainability

This chapter considers why social leaders need to understand the broad concept of sustainability in ECEC and support it through their social leadership. We address the following questions:

- What do we understand by sustainability?
- Why must social leaders champion sustainability?
- How can social leaders amplify the relevance of sustainability to ECEC?

What do we understand by sustainability?

Sustainability is word used freely and, in many contexts, but the word itself describes a complex concept. Nowadays it is most often used with regards to the protection and conservation of the natural environment and our fear about the sustainability of economic growth in the face of natural resource exhaustion and environmental pollution.

The earliest formal articulation of sustainability of resources was a study entitled 'Scarcity and Growth', published originally in 1963 and updated in 2011 by Harold Barnett and Chandler Morse. Responding to these concerns in the 1980s, the World Conservation Strategy (WCS) was formed with the objective of integrating economic and environmental management. However, WCS was unsuccessful in getting world leaders to understand the importance of coordinated economic policies to address the emerging issues. The United Nations responded and formed the Brundtland Commission in 1983, led by Gro Harlem Brundtland, the former Norwegian prime minister. The resulting report in 1987, 'Our Common Future', also known as the Brundtland Report, helped address the issue of the definition of sustainability. By then there were several definitions of sustainability increasingly used to reference everything from locally sourced food to recycling. Santone (2019) commented on how the term had also been somewhat confusingly used by businesses in the context of growth and profits which could be an oxymoron given that some businesses' growth and profits depended on using up more of the world's natural resources. Santone concludes however, that the Brundtland Report was a landmark in highlighting the three Es of sustainability: environmental regeneration and stewardship, economic prosperity and equitable societies. The Commission's definition of sustainability is:

> *development that meets the needs of the present without compromising the ability of future generations to meet their own needs.*

Agyeman (2005) further extended the definition by focusing on it through a systems lens where sustainability allows all species to thrive now and, in the future, in an equitable way within the means of the environment. This description helps us see how the economy and our natural resources are firmly interlinked and underpinned by fairness and this is important if we begin to think of ourselves as guardians of our children's future.

The foreword by Director of UNESCO Dr Irina Bokova to the *Shaping the Future Report* in 2014 was a powerful contribution just as negotiations were being concluded on the global post-2015 agenda to launch the set of sustainable development goals. Bokova highlights the role of education in achieving sustainability:

> *Deep economic and social inequalities, environmental degradation, biodiversity loss, disruption caused by natural disasters and climate change are a litmus test for the global community. More than ever, this is a time when education can – and must – play a decisive role in providing learners across the world with the knowledge, skills and values to discover solutions to today's sustainability challenges. This carries benefit for present and future generations.*
>
> (p. 4)

In 2015, the United Nations General Assembly designed the Sustainable Development Goals (SDGs). These are seventeen interlinked global goals designed to be a 'blueprint to achieve a better and more sustainable future for all'. The SDGs have been both criticized and praised because while they touch on all areas of the human enterprise on earth and highlight the importance of strong principles such as equality and fairness, there were also considerations that such a broad approach may be hard to achieve. In July 2017 the SDGs were made more 'actionable' by a UN Resolution adopted by the General Assembly laying out specific targets for each goal, along with indicators, an SDG tracker to measure progress and an ambitious completion target of 2030.

Figure 6.1 UN Sustainable Development Goals.
https://www.un.org/sustainabledevelopment/ The content of this publication has not
been approved by the United Nations and does not reflect the views of the United
Nations or its officials or Member States.

All the SDGs are structurally relevant to ECEC across the world. For example,
we understand the negative impact of poverty on every child, and we commit
to ensuring that no child goes hungry or must drink dirty water or grow up in
areas of war and conflict. Some of the SDGs also explicitly address the need for
ECEC. For example, SDG number 4 requires us to ensure inclusive and equitable
quality education and the promotion of lifelong learning opportunities for all.
Woodhead (2006) noted that this greatly strengthens the argument for serious
investment in ECEC, so that all children can access high-quality educational
provision from the earliest days of their lives. The specific targets for achieving
SDG 4, as laid out in the SDG tracker, include equal access to high quality pre-
primary education, education for sustainable development and global citizenship
and affordable access to vocational training. These are three particular areas of
importance in ECEC. Education is a powerful pathway to sustainability, but it
depends on adults who understand how to integrate sustainability into every
element of their leadership, pedagogy and operational practice. Sustainability is
not a subject or part of an environmental programme. It is central to the child's
whole experience and needs to be part of a broad and inclusive quality education
(Corlett & O'Sullivan, 2021).

Today, conversations about sustainability are often framed around the idea of
the triple bottom line. Social leaders talk about the importance of aligning the

vision of the organization with the value-led approach that fosters high levels of employee well-being, social and ecological sustainability and viable financial performance. For social leaders in ECEC there is an immediate imperative to build the kind of world we want our children and grandchildren to inherit.

At LEYF, we talk about this within the concept of the social enterprise model. We see this model with its triple bottom line as a way of building the future of ECEC where social and ecological sustainability can be obtained and maintained within the context of acceptable profitability and revenue growth. For example, the purpose of profit at LEYF is to invest in staff and provide more accessible and affordable places for children living with disadvantage and poverty. Having the well qualified staff team is the driver for providing the quality of pedagogy that children need to thrive. While LEYF as a social enterprise is very clear about its triple bottom line, this approach can be used by any ECEC setting that can identify how the economic model is supporting the social purpose and what efforts are being made to underpin the business approach with clear environmental processes and practice.

There is concern that many private companies are attempting to integrate the triple bottom line in their strategic plans and spend large marketing budgets to convince their customers of their dedication to sustainability and solving social problems. However, this alone doesn't deliver sustainability and we need to be alert to the genuine moral integrity of their responses or whether it is what is described as 'greenwashing' whereby the organization or the business present an environmentally responsible public image that does not reflect what is actually happening inside the organization.

Social leaders need to be able to demonstrate that it is possible to run ECEC in a way that places social and environmental sustainability on par with profitability. It is possible. Models like LEYF and Indigo are among many which understand how to run a profitable childcare business where social purpose is key. However, Alice Sharp, Zaridah Abu Zarin and Chantal Williams all agree that while they are not constituted as a social enterprise, they operate their businesses with social purpose at the heart. For example Alice Sharp talks about how she actively recruits students from disadvantaged backgrounds, recounting the empathy needed by social leaders to respond to students living in poverty:

> *for instance one of the students couldn't afford to buy food and so we worked out a system that when she came in and she hadn't had breakfast she would indicate to one of the staff team, who would then go and leave her a packed lunch in the bathroom and she wouldn't have to ask for it and it wouldn't be embarrassing bit she could put it in her bag and join the other students.*

Zaridah Abu Zarin also reflected on her business approach, realizing that she was more closely aligned in her principles and practices with social enterprise than with private business:

> *I think that in Malaysia education has been turned into business. Although money is still important to being a business, I never realised that I'm actually a social enterprise. How stupid I've been! I thought I had to be registered [to count as a social enterprise] but it's actually about the way I work and how I use my profit to subsidise some children. I refused to become a franchise, even though I was encouraged by government, because although I would earn more money, I thought I would lose control of the quality and the freedom to support some children and the coaching I give for free. I would not want to stop that.*

Chantal Williams brings her cautionary tale to bear when she talks about balancing a vision with financial sustainability:

> *In 2011 it all came crashing down. It was awful, it was just the worst time of my life. We ended up doing a mass shutdown of services that weren't profitable. We just got too big too quickly because we wanted to achieve in our vision of providing care where no one else would or does. The question is – why don't they do that already? One of the reasons would be that it isn't profitable. You can call the business a social enterprise or as they say here in Australia, a not for profit, but no one does a business not for profit. You have to make a profit otherwise the business fails, whether you're a social enterprise or not.*

While social leaders are positive about focusing on the triple bottom line we need to consider how that translates into delivering a pedagogy of sustainability. Bell (2016) argues that unless twenty-first-century education is looked at through the lens of sustainability, we will miss what is most important. This is the perfect time in ECEC to instil the values and behaviours of sustainability. Social leaders challenge the view that very young children are unable to understand their environment and the concept of ecological sustainability. We must give children a voice within the sustainability agenda. ECEC is a natural starting point and children are much more competent and thoughtful than we give them credit. Indeed, if sustainable development is relevant to children's lives, then we need to prepare them for their role in dealing with problems they are facing.

Sowing the seeds of sustainability in ECEC starts with a clear shared understanding of what we mean by sustainability. We must avoid the risks noted by Venkataraman (2009) that sustainability becomes an environmental education without setting it in the broader context of socio-cultural factors and the socio-political issues of equity, poverty, democracy and quality of life. He makes a clear distinction between environmental education and education for sustainable development, explaining that environmental education focuses on the human's relationship with the natural world and on ways to conserve, preserve it and properly steward its resources. Teaching and learning about sustainability though require us to teach by finding a balance between economic, social development and environmental care. Thus, while environmental education may well have a place in ECEC, social leaders pay far more attention to embedding sustainability through their social pedagogies.

So what does this look like? Santone (2019) suggests that educating for sustainability involves teaching and learning collective problem-solving skills to address critical environmental, economic and social issues. In 2018, the Cloud Institute talked about education for sustainability as a transformative learning process that equips students, teachers and school systems with the new knowledge and ways of thinking we need to achieve economic prosperity and responsible citizenship while restoring the health of the living systems upon which our lives depend. Thus, sustainability in the context of ECEC pedagogies is about both what you learn about (environmental, economic and social challenges that we all face) and how you learn (through collective problem-solving and collaborative innovation). Everyone must engage in this co-learning together since adult professionals cannot be positioned in this space as 'the expert'. We must start with a recognition that adults have not yet achieved sustainable ways of living and that our hope lies in the contributions of children and young people in finding new ways to think, live, be and do.

Why must social leaders champion sustainability?

Education is the most powerful path to sustainability. Economic and technological solutions, political regulations or financial incentives are not enough. We need fundamental change in the way that we think and act.

(Bokova's forward in UNESCO, 2014)

Social leadership in ECEC means leading with a social purpose and creating a culture that shapes an organization, a service or a pedagogical approach which will foster a fairer society for children and is underpinned by a triple bottom line of economic, social and environmental sustainability to deliver a measurable social impact. To do this, social leaders must believe that ECEC is socially transformative if children are given a voice about their future, as the smallest voices will suffer the biggest impact. Sustainability is holistic. It is about the health and education of our children and relates to every part of their lives. We cannot continue to treat our earth with such disregard and force our children to inherit the predicted catastrophic 2050. Those of us leading in ECEC have a duty to future proof as much as possible and learn how to tread lightly on the planet.

If we are to make a difference in the current state of the world, education is the starting point. It is at all levels of education that ideals of a sustainable future can be instilled. The concept of sustainable development has set in motion a course that we cannot ignore. Education is not the whole answer to every problem, but according to Rogers (2005) education in its broadest sense must play a vital part in all our efforts to imagine and create new relations among people and to foster greater respect for the needs of the environment.

Social leaders must therefore tell the story of sustainability in ECEC. We need to explain, ideally through stories, that sustainability is not just about climate change or reducing plastic usage but is about how we disrupt the existing systems which prevent children accessing quality education. It requires leaders to continue to challenge governments and big business about the continued under-investment in ECEC and particularly in the development of the professionals upon whom the sector depends.

In the UK, access to affordable high-quality childcare is inconsistent. The system is underfunded and the reliance on the market does not guarantee a model that ensures disadvantaged children can access the service that could benefit their overall development with beneficial impact. It reinforces inequality rather than provides a step out of it. London – where LEYF operates – has the highest rate of child poverty of any English region, with 37 per cent (700,000 children) living in poverty. According to the Child Action Poverty Group, the main drivers of child poverty in London are the high housing costs, lack of affordable childcare, low pay and a lack of flexible, part-time jobs. Childcare in London is 28 per cent more expensive than the British average for the under-fives, and costs are rising faster than in any other region. Disadvantaged children start school behind their more advantaged peers, and the gap in performance widens as they progress through the education system.

Staff in the UK also find themselves operating in a sector that is poorly paid and low status. The Education Policy Institute report by Bonetti (2019) confirmed this situation that a large proportion of childcare staff are struggling financially because pay is low in both relative and absolute terms and that childcare staff earned about 40 per cent less than the average female workers and many (44.5 per cent) were claiming state benefits or tax credits which was also borne out by a survey conducted by Nursery World in September 2019.

Social leaders at the helm of organizations can address some of this unfairness by creating a sustainable business model, balancing economic profits, employee well-being and social and ecological sustainability. While in the UK, this tends to be mostly the private and voluntary sector, it does not preclude the state sector which also needs to apply the principles of the triple bottom line even if the funding comes mostly through Government state funds. Mark Carney (2020), the previous Head of the Bank of England, has emphasized the importance of values-led business, as critical to building a better world. He refers to the negative impact as we move from a market economy to a market society that tramples our values because the market cannot value what it does not price. He argues for a new type of leadership that will rebuild public trust which could deliver a more mission-orientated form of capitalism where markets are powerful organizing forces that can be harnessed for good. He suggests a new social contract founded on fairness, personal responsibility, sustainability and solidarity with those values embedded in this reformed market economy. In many ways he is preparing the road for a more hybrid approach to business where the emphasis is doing business by doing good. While this fits very much with the social enterprise model, other businesses can operate in the same way but need to be explicit as to their social purpose and how their leadership balances their economic, social and environmental approaches. As already mentioned, people are alert to the use of greenwashing which would be a negative challenge for any social leader.

While social enterprises share in common the triple bottom line, each social enterprise has its own rich history of how it came into being. In the following case study, Peter Frampton and his colleagues at Learning Enrichment Foundation (LEF) in Ontario Canada reflect on their journey to becoming a social enterprise.

Case Study

The social enterprise model of the Learning Enrichment Foundation

40 odd years ago, before Toronto became one big city or we existed – there was a little city called the city of York. And it was sort of the rust belt. It had been the poorest or second poorest area in the Province and had been that way for 40–50 years. It was the industrial hub and all the businesses were leaving and

the School Board had a £50K surplus and they didn't want to give it back to the Government, and so they created the Learning Enrichment Foundation in the hopes to raise money to run programmes for at risk kids in school. It always had a community economic social enterprise bent to it. The leaders were kind of hard-wired for that.

The first programme was community theatre in order to get to know the community and that led very quickly to a partnership with Levi Strauss and industrial sewing, which led very quickly to construction training and we actually fixed up the navy league and the city's community centre, and then we did store front renovation all along Eglington Hill and that was that economic development framework playing out again.

The City of York was always innovative because it never had any money. And so when childcare was just starting at that point, we had nursery schools but we didn't really have childcare. We opened up our first three childcare centres in high schools so that teen mums could continue their education and you could build clear paths to the sector. And therefore almost all of our centres except for two are in schools and that was a new thing for the City of York.

When we grew to 8 centres, the food was terrible. We rented out the basement of a church and we brought six residential stoves – you could not do this now – and started cooking the meals. But if you're cooking the meals, you might as well train people. And so we started to train people to cook.

Then we moved into our location at 116 Industry Street, and it was to be a business incubator. We had about 10 small businesses, but we were going to lose our shirts pretty quickly, so we brought all the programmes together under one hub. Out of that grew the integrated model, and out of that space grew the town square and that strengthened our connections to the community.

So LEF is a series of failed aspirations and business plans that have all ended brilliantly anyway, just not the way we ever expected. It really is the best way of describing it, and I tell that to MBA students when they come in. We don't bother with feasibility studies, there's more than enough poverty, or needs assessment, because there's more than enough poverty. We don't do feasibility studies because it's always cheaper just to start something quietly than dream about what it might be. And what we do focus on is operational – how do things tie together, how do you bring that kind of efficiency together?

And we don't have a strategic plan. We have four strategic directions. That's it. And it's undated. As soon as it becomes irrelevant, we'll create a new one. It's someone else that pointed it out to me that we never dated it. So it's our five year plan but it can just go on. That gives us the flexibility.

We recently sold our one building and bought two apartments, and we'll be tearing those down and turning them into about 200 units of affordable housing and supported housing. It's always been broad based. We're probably the only childcare organisation in the province that doesn't have children's development in our mission statement, but of course the long-term strategy is childcare. That's how you impact the next generation, and you have to have the quality and you've got to have the right pedagogy, that matters. But it starts from community renewal and I would say it's the long-term strategy and our most effective aspect.

And then most of our staff have been hired through our programmes and so, we hire our graduates and then we grow them – or they grow their own careers, but we're trying to open up those possibilities. So, we've been laying those sorts of frameworks. That's the best way to describe childcare within the LEF context. It's community renewal which needs many responses. You've got to have training for jobs, you've got to be able to welcome and integrate new Canadians, that's huge for us in Toronto. You need the soft supports, the hard supports in terms of skills. You need places for people to practise those skills and none of it happens without childcare and then childcare becomes its own sector and engine.

How can social leaders amplify the relevance of sustainability to ECEC?

Today's leaders face constant change and chaos as they navigate the implications of a global world which connects using social media and digital communication. One of the particular challenges for leaders is how to respond in a world of social media where the issues of facts, feelings and opinions collide to make it harder to know what we should do for the best. Social leaders need to understand the different politico-economic and social contexts and do their best to make informed decisions which will benefit ECEC. Complex issues such as sustainability are contested and getting facts is now much more problematic than simply relying on reading a book. It means social leaders need to be constantly listening, learning, investigating, reading, thinking and reflecting and be willing to engage with a diverse group of thinkers in order to make decisions that positively benefit children.

According to Fullan and Quinn (2016), the mark of an educated person is that of a thinking doer and a doer who thinks. Social leaders are often associated with learning by doing and addressing sustainability may require that frame of mind where they learn to do and do to learn. Whatever we do, social leaders must be impatient with lack of action. Social leaders need to be impatient and willing to jump into the complexities of an issue. Sustainability is certainly one of those issues.

Jacqueline Lamb, CEO of Indigo Childcare Group, describes the urgency of the social leader:

I run at 150 miles per hour and sometimes you just need to pull me back a little bit. You're a social entrepreneur and so you're going all the time – there's chaos, but you have to give order to people. You see such challenge and such unfairness out there and so much drama out there – you think, there's isn't time for us to draw breath. For some of them, we're their only hope.

One way to highlight the relevance of sustainability in ECEC is to use the SDGs as a framework with examples of actions we can take in ECEC. SDGs provide the knowledge needed to promote sustainability which is too big an issue to tackle in one attempt. Everyone needs a stepped plan to move to a position of action so that ultimately every aspect of the organization is as sustainable as possible. Options such as accreditation programmes and inspection systems with specific measures may also help to shape the plan and make the conversation with parents easier. Social leaders must also tell the story of each step explaining the full rationale for each action to engage all stakeholders and enable them to campaign for and support every effort.

The ultimate purpose of the SDGs is to ensure that every child has access to quality ECEC as a means of giving them a fair chance in life from the start. Understanding how we create a sustainable ECEC needs us to understand what sustainability looks like from our vision and operational platform to our measures and organizational culture. Ultimately, sustainability means creating a model which allows children to thrive now and in the future within the resources of the environment. The following are suggestions to begin the conversation with colleagues and supporters and to raise awareness. Cheryl Hadland (2020, p. 2) put it succinctly when she said:

Sustainability is a complex subject. Every decision will come with counter arguments. The best anyone can do is be pragmatic and make the most informed decision they can at the time. Be prepared to reflect and to continuously try to improve what you do. Inevitably, you will make some mistakes along the way, and that's normal. That's how we learn after all

The SDGs are a helpful framework to align your own sustainability goals, however, given there are seventeen, you may choose not to focus on all of them to begin with, but on those that feel most immediately relevant. To help you start to think more about this we have looked at each one and given an example of how they relate to ECEC. We recognize that the examples and evidence used to illustrate connections between ECEC and each SDG below are predominantly based in the UK. Your national context may be different and change how you think about the relationship between each SDG and ECEC.

SDG 1: 'No poverty'

This is a huge task, but social leaders in ECEC can lead sector conversations about why child poverty must be addressed urgently. Child poverty is an issue children and families face, even in the context of relatively rich countries, such as the UK, where one in four children live in families which, according to the Social Metrics Commission (2020), earn 55 per cent of the median income. Work is considered the way out of poverty but according to Hick and Lanau (2017) 60 per cent of people within the poverty category are working. In the UK, ECEC operates within a dual policy response to poverty. One is that access to affordable childcare is essential so families can work and the second is that high-quality ECEC can support children who are disadvantaged by poverty and family circumstances. The Effective Preschool, Primary and Secondary Education (EPPSE) study found a robust link between experiences of high-quality ECEC and long-term educational outcomes, and the correlation was strongest for children from backgrounds of disadvantage.

However, to deliver both those policies the ECEC sector needs sufficient funding to provide the affordable, accessible and high-quality places necessary. Childcare needs to be affordable to enable parents to work and that is not currently the case. Reports from Early Years Alliance (2018) show that in the UK we are continually operating with a shortfall of over £500million and the consequences are that fewer places are available to the children from disadvantaged families as there are not enough organizations operating a sustainable business model to provide the places necessary. According to the Sutton Trust report (2021), the situation has been severely aggravated by the Covid pandemic.

SDG 2: Zero hunger

The role of ECEC in helping children not go hungry is significant. The first indications of societal shifts and emerging problems are often noticed among our youngest children. We have watched the rise of Food Banks in the UK and across Europe, but the issues of hunger were fully spotlighted during the Covid pandemic. For example, according to the Trussell Trust (2021) between 1 April 2020 and 31 March 2021, food banks in their UK wide network distributed 2.5 million emergency food parcels to people in crisis, a 33 per cent increase on the previous year and 980,000 of these went to children. Many ECEC settings run their own Food Banks or support local ones and while this is not a long-term solution to hunger, they are supporting families by providing nutritious healthy food while continuing to stress the importance of food for small children.

SDG 3: Good health and well-being

The UK and much of the world is facing a crisis in child obesity. The consequences of obesity for young children and the economic, health and social cost of this crisis are serious. Children who are obese are at risk of being obese into adulthood and developing heart disease, diabetes, asthma and other serious illness. Starting to address this in ECEC is essential through a range of activities including better food, more informed chefs, better understanding of physical development and a partnership with organizations addressing the wider obesogenic environment. In a written reflection on her life as a social leader in ECEC, Anne Patterson reflected on the impact of interconnectedness and understanding what we do as humans impacts on each other.

> *This matters as humanity will continue to be challenged by numerous interconnected environmental, social and economic issues: It is important that children get to know the community that they live in and the people that live there give them a sense of belonging – a sense of 'linkedness'.*

SDG 4: Quality education

What constitutes quality is the subject of much debate and discussion. We know that quality ECEC is essential especially for children who are from disadvantaged backgrounds. We create a double disadvantage if they do not receive the best and highest quality education (OECD, 2019). Our role is to continually improve the delivery of the service and ensure we are constantly striving to improve the underlying structures that together make quality. For example, at LEYF we believe our Social Pedagogy is central to our quality along with the training opportunities we offer staff. This fits with the views of our social leaders who generally agree that quality needs skilled staff, properly deployed with generous adult to child ratios and who can deliver a clearly articulated and well-understood pedagogy within an environment that supports their practice and helps build harmonious relationships and strong and engaged partnerships with parents.

SDG 5: Gender equality

One approach to addressing equality in ECEC is to examine why the sector is so disproportionally female. According to the Education Policy Institute report (2020) the number of male workers in the childcare sector in the UK has increased yet remains very low at 7.4 per cent. This is only around half the proportion of male workers in other female-dominated professions, such as hairdressers and beauticians (13.7 per cent) and with nursery and primary teachers (15.8 per cent). Campaigns to include more men in childcare have been led by many ECEC social leaders but in a way that ensures the value of the female workforce is not diminished so that ensuring more men in the sector is not perceived as them riding in on their white chargers to save us. Alice Sharp from Experiential Play in Glasgow has been working with fathers for many years including running specific programmes to help them consider working in the Early Years. In this short case study she provides a little more depth about her rationale.

Case Study
The 'Dads' Group
Alice Sharp, CEO of Experiential Play, Scotland

Our project came from many conversations, and I had been engaged with the work LEYF was doing to encourage men into childcare. But every time I was speaking to my head-teacher colleagues they talked about how important it was to get Dads involved in the day to day work of the nursery and especially as they had been really successful in getting them to volunteer. So, we decided to do something about that. I went to Glasgow City Council and convince them to provide some funding to identify a few Dads, which we did and then we agreed to see whether there was any interest. We had a meeting with the

City Council and invited four head teachers to each bring a Dad to a meeting, and I brought a Dad as well.

We agreed that our training would be a male only cohort. We did a lot of interviews and formed a group of 15 Dads. For a year it was just the men completing a qualification. It was hard work, there's no doubt about it, we did enrichment, we took them to the island of Iona, we talked about beauty – it was really interesting and we loved that work. We did have some drop out, but that was mostly because the Dads were trying to do a job and a qualification at the same time. We resolved some issues by working with the Benefits Agency to agree that those on benefit didn't have to turn up and apply for jobs because they were volunteering in the nurseries full-time, and they were paid nothing. They got their benefits for the duration no questions. It was a huge fight to get that! But there were some Dads that weren't on benefits. They had jobs in kitchens, one worked as a waiter, one did some voluntary and paid work in a care home. And they couldn't give those jobs up so it became too much – therefore the majority of people that dropped out of the qualification did so because they were having to balance feeding their families and trying to change their lives.

Despite that, four of them are now doing the Early Years Degree – their whole perspective, their aspirations have changed dramatically and if the head teachers hadn't identified them as having a spark and we hadn't have found funding to make that happen, they would still be living the life they were living. That continuous cycle would not have been broken. It has been incredibly successful yet getting funding for it again has been a problem. We don't have a Dads' groups at the moment, we don't have a Mums' group either because Glasgow City Council has no funding to allocate. And I know that there's no point going straight to Government because we're a limited company and we will come up against barriers. It's a shame because the Government money often goes to the colleges to get more men into childcare, yet they have struggled to recruit. I don't understand why it failed because we made it happen before.

But that said I'm really positive about the whole sector – of course there are all those challenges but you just get on with it. That's the type of leaders that we are, in that you throw something at me, and I'll just throw it back at you. It's about resilience and pure feisty grit because we can see how we can make a difference.

SDG 6: Clean water and sanitation

Teaching children about water conservation begins in the nursery. We can take for granted in the UK that we can turn on our taps and out will pour clean fresh water but that is not the case for children in other parts of the world. According to the US charity, *charity:water* 785 million people in the world live without clean water. That's nearly one in ten people worldwide or ten times the population of the UK. The majority live in isolated rural areas and spend hours every day walking to collect water for their family. Not only does walking for water keep children out of school or take up time that parents could be using to earn money, but the water often carries diseases that can make everyone sick. What we can do is to begin by teaching our youngest children that having clean tap water is a privilege and we need to take care not to waste it whether by recycling rainwater in the garden or having taps that don't drip and loos that use less water to flush (grey water) or better still re-using rainwater as an irrigation system, planting drought loving plants and avoiding plastic bottled water.

SDG 7: Affordable and clean electricity

Review your electricity consumption. One simple way to begin is to look at LED lighting replacement. Check the setting for old inefficient lighting, for example, an old-style fluorescent light fitting would burn say 120 watts, while an LED replacement could burn anything up to 60 per cent less and commonly can achieve 45 per cent less energy use. Some areas are commonly over lit, so you could consider Microwave or PIR movement sensors, time clocks or intelligent lighting to further save energy which senses daylight so if there is adequate light from the windows, the lights not needed will turn off, the lights in the back of the room without adequate daylight will remain on. The result is reduced electricity costs and a reduced carbon footprint.

SDG 8: Decent work and economic growth

The ECEC sector is often a low-paid sector. In the UK staff must be paid the minimum national living wage. This is not enough, and we also need to look at ways of providing staff with fair benefits such as a good pension, proper training and development opportunities no matter what type of contract they are on. In the UK the sector is identified by the Low Paid Commission regularly and in their 2020 report they noted that childcare remain underfunded, with low-paid workers within those sectors ultimately bearing the consequences. Covid-19 has only accentuated the long-standing issues in those low-paying sectors where the Government is the main source of funding.

SDG 9: Industry, innovation and infrastructure

In every ECEC setting we can consider our internal audit. This is how we measure our service delivery separate from the financial audit which is the annual external check of our financial management. The ECEC audit can be framed within the SDGs and check what we are doing against each of the goals that is relevant to our own setting. For example, it can be discussed as our approach to environmental stewardship and cross checked against the policies and procedures that guide our actions with respect to buildings, procurement, purchasing, waste prevention and our carbon footprint. Set that within a socially enterprising attitude and skills such as critical thinking, problem-solving, collaboration and creativity, we can build an innovative attitude to solving social problems.

SDG10: Reduced inequalities

The importance of ECEC leading the way in creating inclusive services is not to be under-estimated. Inclusion is often narrowly perceived to be about race, gender and disabilities but it is much more than this and needs the ECEC sector to be fully alert to what it means to deliver inclusion. For example, a report by Simpson examined the attitude ECEC staff had to child poverty. They saw it in two ways: a structural issue caused by economic policies or poverty caused by personal and deviant behaviour rather than wider economic forces. The personal views of how staff perceived poverty impacted on how they interacted with parents, for example, as to whether they considered seeking additional support for the child if they felt the required support would not be continued in the home. It is essential that ECEC settings address these prejudiced perceptions of children living in poverty, ensuring that access to resources and support is equitable.

SDG 11: Sustainable cities and communities

In his book on *Trust*, Anthony Seldon (2009) asked that we make communities greener and cleaner and that we pay rapid attention to litter, and decay. He noted that improved local environments improved behaviour and communal pride. He referenced a long-going campaign to plant more trees in London and delegating a minimum of 20 per cent of land in all urban communities devoted to green space for gardens and recreation. This reminds me of a piece of research we did at LEYF with the four-year-old children in a fairly rundown neighbourhood. We gave the children disposable cameras and they walked around taking photos. Their photo analysis showed three things they said made them uneasy: litter, dogs and bird guano. This information was fed into the London plan but while dogs are more often on leads these days, the issue of litter remains both overwhelming and disturbing.

SDG12: Responsible consumption and production

Most ECEC settings provide children with food. ECEC settings like LEYF develop a Chef Academy to train all ECEC chefs to better understand children's nutritional needs, prepare and serve food that is more seasonal and sourced locally and better manage portion sizes and food waste.

SDG13: Climate action

Every ECEC setting can pay attention to the impact of climate change by how they use resources wisely, turn the heating a little lower, pay attention to waste and raise the awareness of the children and families so they can create a ripple effect.

SDG14: Life below water

A simple but effective first step for any ECEC social leader would be to change our practice and ban single use plastic, remove glitter, stop using clingfilm and replace wet wipes. All this would reduce plastic usage and stop it getting onto the oceans with all the damage it does.

SDG15: Life on land

Let's heed the words of Richard Louv (2012) who warns that humans are having a devastating impact on the natural environment and as more than half of the world populations now live in towns and cities, the traditional ways of how human beings have experienced nature are vanishing along with biodiversity.

Children can connect with nature through what Thomas Weaver described as 'the poetry of your back garden'. One very simple idea we use at LEYF is the annual 'wildlife photographer of the year' to encourage children and teachers to interact and take photos of wildlife they find in their gardens or on trips and outings whether a small bug, a speedy squirrel or a noisy parrot! Cassie Holland, Manager at Archfield House Nursery in Bristol, created the 'Bristol Beach Schools' initiative to deeply root children's learning in time spent outdoors in the natural environment of the beach. By connecting with the natural environment, children can build not only their awareness and understanding of nature, but their love of it. This is vital if we are to support children to be advocates for sustainability.

SDG 16: Peace, justice and strong institutions

Some children are growing up in places where there is no peace and ECEC is important in how we can create a safe space for children to grow up together. Pauline Walmsley the CEO of Early Education in Northern Ireland spoke very passionately about the need to understand how ECEC is important in embattled communities. She reflected on the story of the organization and the importance of knowing its roots to connect staff and families with the original vision.

> We have a vision to support children to be emotionally and physically well and respectful of difference. We say that children are strong, confident and must be visible in their own community. This is very important for us in Northern Ireland where children can learn and grow up in a peaceful and shared society. That's the vision of our organisation, and our social purpose is to promote and develop high quality evidence-informed early childhood services for young children and their families. That has remained the purpose of the organisation going back to when our founding mothers met in 1965.
>
> We also provide professional development in relation to advocacy so that settings don't just see themselves as something that's offering a service in a community, but they actually see themselves as a vibrant part of the community – that they're building partnerships within the community, that they're using those partnerships to promote peace.

SDG17: Partnership for the goals

Social leaders need to participate to make a difference at all levels: the child, the family, the workplace, the local community, the national community and through global movements. This requires them to partner with a range of people, organizations and businesses and create an ECEC alliance to tell the stories about how we can better understand and support sustainability which recognizes the interdependencies between societies, economies and the environment and weave it into the ECEC pedagogy.

Conclusion

Sustainability is finally moving to the centre of the political and public agenda. This is good news as we face huge global issues including climate change, environmental degradation, water scarcity, biodiversity loss, pollution, food insecurity and food waste, poverty and disease. This may seem completely disconnected from the world of ECEC but a central tenet of our work is to prepare children to undertake their roles and responsibilities as accountable global citizens.

Social leaders build leadership for sustainability through strategies, culture, operational processes and practice and partnerships, that can improve the quality and impact of a sustainable development within the organization's ecosystem. Social leaders seek sustainable change, regardless of role or position to build the kind of world that we want to live in and that we want our children to inherit. This requires us to understand and operate within complex interconnected and dynamic economic, social and environmental systems.

To do this, social leaders also need to be willing to complete their own personal journey of discovery centred around a compassionate and empathetic understanding of sustainability. Solutions for a sustainable, flourishing world require a new model of ECEC leadership that can foster a sustainability mindset. One that places economic, social and environmental sustainability at the heart of the service and ensures we pass on a flourishing world that is better than the one we inherited to a future generation.

7

Conclusion

Social leadership: Our commitment to ECEC's social purpose

In this final chapter, we want to take some time to consider:

1. The main arguments that we've put forward in the book and their implications.
2. The contribution that this model can make to leadership research and practice in ECEC.
3. Next steps for how we can grow our knowledge, understanding and practice of social leadership in ECEC.

We hope that this chapter reverberates with the hope and optimism that we feel for ECEC. We are part of a sector that plays a crucial role in shaping society. We can influence society for the better when we adopt models of leadership and leadership development that put this social purpose at the very heart of everything we do.

The social leadership vision: A summary

The model of social leadership in ECEC involves six interwoven elements, which you will have read about in detail in the previous chapters:

1. Leading with social purpose
2. Driving a social pedagogy
3. Creating a culture of collaborative innovation
4. Investing in others' leadership
5. Facilitating powerful conversations
6. Sowing the seeds of sustainability

These six elements have emerged from the ongoing work of London Early Years Foundation (LEYF) and dialogues with global leaders in ECEC, all committed to creating a fairer society through the vehicle of ECEC. The six elements are the levers for change, through which leaders can become social leaders.

We suggest that leadership development programmes, whether they are part of a degree-level offer, job-embedded professional development or a stand-alone course, can use these elements as the basis for transformation. While we have explained the elements as self-contained components, it would make sense for the development of social leaders to begin with the first and second elements: social purpose and a social pedagogy. There is no social leadership without social purpose; it is the least negotiable element of the model. However, social leaders need to articulate the social purpose that focuses their work and drives their pedagogy. There is no 'one-size-fits-all' approach and a deep understanding of context will resonate through the articulation of social purpose. Once the social purpose is clear, a social pedagogy becomes the essential vehicle. For us the social purpose is the heart, a social pedagogy is the heartbeat.

The third, fourth and fifth elements of the model relate to organizational culture. It is where social leaders define their vision and drive it through their organization, through the people, the processes and the practice. Social leaders embrace ECEC in their own organizations but also strive to create an ECEC community across the globe. The model therefore places a great deal of emphasis on culture-building as a means for change. Finally, sowing the seeds of sustainability is just that; we must do more to get to grips with not just the climate crisis, but the ferocious inequalities that impact our youngest children and blight their futures. Sustainability is about finding a pathway to a better future and social leaders in ECEC light the way.

Our contribution

Of course, there are caveats to the model that we have produced. Our intention is not to produce a static model ripe for intensive evaluation. Instead, we offer the model as a starting point for the powerful conversations that are the focus of the fifth element. There are many limitations shaping what we are offering in this book and it is right and proper to acknowledge those here.

While our model is based on conversations with global leaders in ECEC, we wholeheartedly recognize and embrace the need for more diversity in the leadership voices that influence how we think about social leadership. We have focused, by and large, on leaders in countries that are relatively high on the development index but who also have recognizable problems in their ECEC delivery. The model would benefit greatly from conversations that go beyond these parameters and think about how (and if) the social leadership model feels relevant in other parts of the world and in alternative ECEC contexts, for example, those that do not rely so heavily on the mixed economy model that has impacted most of our interviewees.

Is social leadership the only way to think about leadership in ECEC? Of course not. However, we hope you agree that there are far too few conversations about leadership and leadership development in the context of ECEC. We have much more to learn about leadership specifically designed for the sector. At the very least, our model of social leadership is an agitation for more thinking and storytelling about leadership in ECEC. A fabulous outcome of the book would be the conceptualization among readers of alternative models that feel and prove to be more appropriate in their specific contexts. We are not precious about the social leadership model; what we are precious about is the role that ECEC leadership has to play in creating fairer and better societies.

In the same vein, this book does not offer an evaluation of the social leadership model. It is not a careful assessment of whether the six elements we have identified comprehensively describe and explain the work of social leaders in ECEC. It is something far more fluid, based largely on the leaders' stories of the messy realities of the sector. It is an exploration based on warm conversations, alive with laughter, about what 'feels right'. In this sense, the bias is inevitable, but we remain convinced that the account we provide can be useful and valid as a means for supporting leadership and leadership development across ECEC.

We fully recognize that the problems and issues of ECEC are largely systemic. The chronic under-investment in ECEC across so many nations of the world is truly unacceptable. We are not painting a vision of social leaders as superheroes who can save the day by 'making a silk purse from a sow's ear' (to use an English saying from the mid-1500s). In each of the chapters, we have highlighted how the work of the social leader in ECEC is not simply about doing your best in the context of a rotten system. Instead, it is about making genuine social change and doing this in both small and big ways. There is a dynamic relationship between individuals working in the sector and the systems that operate at a national and even international level. We can bring about systemic change, but only if we are prepared to foster cultures of collaborative innovation and facilitate powerful conversations that ripple across ECEC. The model of social leadership is therefore both internal and external. It is more than effectively leading the internal operations of an organization. It is about the external voice: the willingness to build collaboration through conversations, trust and openness.

Next steps for research

Undoubtedly, we need more research to understand how the model of social leadership presented here resonates (or not) in different contexts around the world. We need this research to develop the model and its potential impact. We also need to extend the methodologies of research that we bring to these investigations. While we believe passionately in the power of conversations, observations are also important. We need to investigate if what people have said marries with what actually happens. This is particularly important for those elements of the model that focus on culture. For example, we need to understand, with more fine-grained detail, how and if collaborative innovation is alive every day in the most routine and mundane moments and whether it is essential for empowering leaders to make shifts in culture and outcomes.

Next steps for practice

We hope that our emphasis on conversations will be taken up in the ways in which the social leadership model is used and disseminated. The social leadership model is not about individuals making change by themselves. It is about creating and nourishing communities of practice that can foster social leadership across the sector. We want to see professional development programmes and initiatives that connect the social leadership model in an authentic and immediate way to practice.

A final note

In his later writings, Paolo Freire suggests the need for 'just ire'. Just ire is anger that works to create, rather than destroy. When we look at the situation of ECEC around the world – not everywhere, but certainly in most places – there is much to feel 'just ire' about. Writing from the UK in 2021, we are angry at the under-valuing of ECEC in this nation and the iniquitous consequences for children and young families. Anger is not enough. It is a starting point for change and innovation and we humbly offer the model of social leadership as a creative response to our just ire. We bring it to the table with optimism and a deep willingness for collaborative re-workings based on an inclusive engagement with diverse voices across ECEC across the globe.

@JuneOSullivan
@DrMonaSakr

References

Agyeman, J. (2005) Alternatives for Community and Environment: Where Justice and Sustainability Meet. *Environment: Science and Policy for Sustainable Development*, 47(6), 10–23.

Agyeman, J., Bullard, R. D. & Evans, B. (Eds.) (2003) *Just Sustainabilities: Development in an Unequal World*. Cambridge, MA: MIT Press.

Anders, Y. (2015) *Literature Review on Pedagogy*. Paris: OECD.

Arbour, M., Yoshikawa, H., Atwood, S., Duran Mellado, F. R., Godoy Ossa, F., Trevino Villareal, E. & Snow, C. E. (2016) *Improving Quality and Child Outcomes in Early Childhood Education by Redefining the Role Afforded to Teachers in Professional Development: A Continuous Quality Improvement Learning Collaborative among Public Preschools in Chile*. Evanston, IL: Society for Research on Educational Effectiveness.

Aubrey, C., Godfrey, R. & Harris, A. (2013) How Do They Manage? An Investigation of Early Childhood Leadership. *Educational Management Administration & Leadership*, 41(1), 5–29.

Aynsley-Green, A. (2018) *The British Betrayal of Childhood. Challenging Uncomfortable Truths and Bringing about Change*. London: Routledge.

Baker, W. F. & O'Malley, M. (2008) *Leading with Kindness: How Good People Consistently Get Superior Results*. New York, NY: AMACOM.

Barnett, H. & Morse, C. (2011) *Scarcity and Growth : The Economics of Natural Resource Availability*. London: Routledge.

Bell, D. V. (2016) Twenty First Century Education: Transformative Education for Sustainability and Responsible Citizenship. *Journal of Teacher Education for Sustainability*, 18(1), 48–56.

Bertram, T., Pascal, C., Goodman, D., Irvine, A. & Parr, J. (2019) Pedagogic Systems Leadership within Complex and Changing ECEC Systems. In S. Cheesman & M. Reed (Eds.) *Pedagogies for Leading Practice*. (pp. 182–204). London: Routledge.

Bertrand, P., Guegan, J., Robieux, L., McCall, C. A. & Zenasni, F. (2018) Learning Empathy through Virtual Reality: Multiple Strategies for Training Empathy-related Abilities Using Body Ownership Illusions in Embodied Virtual Reality. *Frontiers in Robotics and AI*, 5, 26.

Bonetti, S. (2019) *The Early Years Workforce in England*. London: Education Policy Institute. Accessed 13.07.2021: https://epi.org.uk/publications-and-research/the-early-years-workforce-in-england/

Bonetti, S. (2020) *Early Years Workforce Development in England: Key Ingredients and Missed Opportunities*. London: Education Policy Institute. Accessed online: file:///C:/Users/mona5/Downloads/Early_years_workforce_development_EPI.pdf

Bottery, M. (2004) *The Challenges of Educational Leadership*. London: Sage.

Boud, D. & Hager, P. (2012) Re-thinking Continuing Professional Development through Changing Metaphors and Location in Professional Practices. *Studies in Continuing Education*, 34(1), 17–30.

Brint, S. (2001) Gemeinschaft Revisited: A Critique and Reconstruction of the Community Concept. *Sociological Theory*, 19(1), 1–23.

Brühlmeier, A. (2010) *Head, Heart and Hand. Education in the Spirit of Pestalozzi*. Cambridge: Sophia Books.

Bruner, J. (1990) *Acts of Meaning: Four Lectures on Mind and Culture*. Cambridge, MA: Harvard University Press.

Bruner, J. (1996) *The Culture of Education*. Cambridge, MA: Harvard University Press.

Bruner, J. (2002) *Making Stories: Law, Literature and Life*. Harvard University Press.

Cameron, C. & Moss, P. (Eds.) (2011) *Social Pedagogy and Working with Children and Young People: Where Care and Education Meet*. London: Jessica Kingsley Publishers.

Carney, M. (2020) *Values: Building a Better World*. London: William Collins.

Ceeda (2019) About Early Years: Sector Skills Survey. Accessed 13.07.2021: https://aboutearlyyears.co.uk/

Charfe, L. & Gardner, A. (2019) *Social Pedagogy and Social Work*. London: Sage.

Charfe, L. & Gardner, A. (2020) 'Does My Haltung Look Big in This?': The Use of Social Pedagogical Theory for the Development of Ethical and Value-led Practice. *International Journal of Social Pedagogy*, 9(1), 11. DOI: https://doi.org/10.14324/111.444.ijsp.2020.v9.x.011

Cheesman, S. & Reed, M. (Eds.) (2019) *Pedagogies for Leading Practice*. London: Routledge.

Cheung, A. et al. (2018) Teachers' Perceptions of the Effect of Selected Leadership Practices on Pre-primary Children's Learning in Hong Kong. *Early Child Development and Care*, 1–19, http://dx.doi.org/10.1080/03004430.2018.1448394.

Cheung, A. C. K., Keung, C. P. C., Kwan, P. Y. K. & Cheung, L. Y. S. (2019) Teachers' Perceptions of the Effect of Selected Leadership Practices on Pre-Primary Children's Learning in Hong Kong. *Early Child Development and Care*, 189(14), 2265–83.

Child Poverty Action Group (2020) Child Poverty Action Group Annual Report. Accessed 13.07.2021: https://cpag.org.uk/sites/default/files/files/page/CPAG-Annual-Report-2019-20.pdf

Cleary, B. (2019) Reinterpreting Bildung in Social Pedagogy. *International Journal of Social Pedagogy*, 8(3), 1–12.

Cleary, B. (2020) Ethics in an Individualized Field of Practice–Social Pedagogy in the Context of the Neoliberal Organization. *International Journal of Social Pedagogy*. Accessed 25.11.2021: https://ucl.scienceopen.com/hosted-document?doi=10.14324/111.444.ijsp.2020.v9.x.004

Cooper, M. (2014) *Cut Adrift: Families in Insecure Times*. Berkeley, CA: University of California Press.

Cooper, M. & Pugh, A. J. (2020) Families across the Income Spectrum: A Decade in Review. *Journal of Marriage and Family*, 82(1), 272–99.

Coram Family and Childcare (2021) Childcare Survey. Accessed 13. 07.2021: https://www.familyandchildcaretrust.org/childcare-survey-2021

Corlett & O'Sullivan (2021) *Sustainability for the Early Years*. London: Bloomsbury.

Coussée, F., Bradt, L., Roose, R. & Bouverne-De Bie, M. (2010) The Emerging Social Pedagogical Paradigm in UK Child and Youth Care: Deus ex machina or Walking the Beaten Path? *The British Journal of Social Work*, 40(3), 789–809.

Craft, A., Cremin, T., Burnard, P., Dragovic, T. & Chappell, K. (2013) Possibility Thinking: Culminative Studies of an Evidence-based Concept Driving Creativity? *Education*, 3–13, 41(5), 538–56.

Cumming, T. & Wong, S. (2019) Towards a Holistic Conceptualisation of Early Childhood Educators' Work-related Well-being. *Contemporary Issues in Early Childhood*, 20(3), 265–81.

Dennis, S. E. & O'Connor, E. (2013) Reexamining Quality in Early Childhood Education: Exploring the Relationship between the Organizational Climate and the Classroom. *Journal of Research in Childhood Education*, 27(1), 74–92.

Department for Education (2015) Effective Pre-School, Primary and Secondary Education Project. Accessed 13.07.2021: https://assets.publishing.service.gov.uk/government/uploads/system/uploads/attachment_data/file/455670/RB455_Effective_pre-school_primary_and_secondary_education_project.pdf.pdf

Dewey, J. (1976) Creative Democracy: The Task before Us. In J. Boydston (Ed.) *John Dewey: The later works, 1925–1953*, Vol. 14. (pp. 224–30). Carbondale, IL: Southern Illinois University Press.

Doepke, M. & Zilibotti, F. (2019) *Love, Money and Parenting*. Princeton, NJ: Princeton University Press.

Douglass, A. (2011) Improving Family Engagement: The Organizational Context and Its Influence on Partnering with Parents in Formal Child Care Settings. *Early Childhood Research & Practice*, 13(2). https://files.eric.ed.gov/fulltext/EJ956369.pdf

Douglass, A. (2017) *Leading for Change in Early Care and Education*. New York: Teachers College Press.

Douglass, A. (2019) Leadership for Quality Early Childhood Education and Care. OECD Working Paper. Accessed 13.07.2021: https://www.oecd-ilibrary.org/education/leadership-for-quality-early-childhood-education-and-care_6e563bae-en

Douglass, A. L. (2019) Leadership for Quality Early Childhood Education and Care. OECD Education Working Paper No. 211. Accessed 02.03.2021: http://www.oecd.org/officialdocuments/publicdisplaydocumentpdf/?cote=EDU/WKP%282019%2919&docLanguage=En

Dweck, C. (2007) *Mindset: The New Psychology of Success*. New York, NY: Ballantine Books.

Early Years Alliance (2018) Families to Foot the Bill as New Figures Reveal Half a Billion Shortfall in Childcare Funding. Accessed 14.07.2021: https://www.eyalliance.org.uk/families-set-foot-bill-new-figures-reveal-half-billion-shortfall-childcare-funding

Early Years Alliance (2020) The Forgotten Sector Report. Accessed 09.07.2021: https://www.eyalliance.org.uk/forgotten-sector-report

Early Years Workforce Commission (2021) A Workforce in Crisis: Saving Our Early Years. Accessed 25.11.2021: https://www.pacey.org.uk/Pacey/media/Website-files/Non-PACEY%20documents%20_PDFs_/a-workforce-in-crisis-saving-our-early-years.pdf

Edmondson, A. (2018) *The Fearless Organization: Creating Psychological Safety in the Workplace for Learning, Innovation and Growth*. Hoboken, NJ: Harvard Business Press.

Education Endowment Foundation (2021) *Covid-19 Disruptions. Attainment Gaps and Primary School Responses*. London: Education Endowment Foundation.

Eichsteller, G. & Holthoff, S. (2011) Social Pedagogy as an Ethical Orientation towards Working with People—Historical Perspectives. *Children Australia*, 36(4), 176–86.

Eichsteller, G. & Holthoff, S. (2012) The Art of Being a Social Pedagogue: Developing Cultural Change in Children's Homes in Essex. *International Journal of Social Pedagogy*, 1, 30–45.

Eriksson, L. (2014) The Understandings of Social Pedagogy from Northern European Perspectives. *Journal of Social Work*, 14(2), 165–82.

Farini, F. (in press) Pedagogical Leadership in Italian Early Childhood Education Settings: Managing Conflicts while Facilitating Participative Decision-making. In M. Sakr & J. O'Sullivan (Eds.) *Pedagogical Leadership in Early Childhood Education: Conversations from across the World*. London: Bloomsbury.

Fielding, M. (2007) On the Necessity of Radical State Education: Democracy and the Common School. *Journal of Philosophy of Education*, 41(4), 539–57.

Freire, P. (1968/1999) *Pedagogy of the Oppressed*. London: Penguin Books.

Freire, P. (2001/1996) *Pedagogy of Freedom: Ethics, Democracy and Civic Courage*. Lanham, MD: Rowman and Littlefield Publishers.

Fullan, M. & Quinn, J. (2016) *Coherence: The Right Drivers in Action for Schools, Districts and Systems*. Thousand Oaks, CA: Corwin.

Garnett, H. (2018) *Developing Empathy*. London: Jessica Kingsley.

Gilbert, J. (2010) Equality and Difference: Schooling and Social Democracy in the 21st Century. *Critical Literacy: Theories and Practices*, 4(1), 66–77.

Gittell, J. (2016) *Transforming Relationships for High Performance: The Power of Relational Coordination*. Stanford, CA: Stanford University Press. [51].

Gittell, J. et al. (2008) Impact of Relational Coordination on Job Satisfaction and Quality Outcomes: A Study of Nursing Homes. *Human Resource Management Journal*, 18(2), 154–70, https://doi.org/10.1111/j.1748-8583.2007.00063.x

Gittell, J., Seidner, R. & Wimbush, J. (2010) A Relational Model of How High Performance Work Systems Work. *Organization Science*, 21(2), 490–506, https://doi.org/10.1287/orsc.1090.0446

Gorski, P., Zenkov, K., Osei-Kofi, N. & Sapp, J. (Eds.) (2013) *Cultivating Social Justice Teachers*. Virginia: Stylus Publications.

Guglielmo, F. & Palsule, S. (2014) *The Social Leader: Redefining Leadership for the Complex Social Age*. Brookline, MA: Bibliomotion.

Hadland, C. (2020) *Creating an Eco-Friendly Early Years Setting*. London: Routledge.

Hämäläinen, J. (2003) The Concept of Social Pedagogy in the Field of Social Work. *Journal of Social Work*, 3(1), 69–80.

Haskins, G., Thomas, M. & Johri, L. (Eds.) (2018) *Kindness in Leadership*. London: Routledge.

Hatton, K. (2013) *Social Pedagogy in the UK: Theory and Practice*. Lyme Regis: Russell House Publishing.

Heckman, J. J. (2015) Four Big Benefits of Investing in Early Childhood Development. The Heckman Equation. Accessed 13.07.2021: https://heckmanequation.org/www/assets/2017/01/F_Heckman_FourBenefitsInvestingECDevelopment_022615.pdf

Henderson, L. (2017) 'Someone Had to Have Faith in Them as Professionals': An Evaluation of an Action Research Project to Develop Educational Leadership across the Early Years. *Educational Action Research*, 25(3), 387–401.

Hick, R. & Lanau, A. (2017) In-Work Poverty in the UK: Problem, Policy Analysis and Platform for Action. Cardiff University. Accessed 14.07.2021: https://www.cardiff.ac.uk/__data/assets/pdf_file/0009/758169/Hick-and-Lanau-In-work-poverty-in-the-UK.pdf

Hickman, G. R. & Sorenson, G. J. (2014) *The Power of Invisible Leadership: How a Compelling Common Purpose Inspires Exceptional Leadership*. London: Sage.

hooks, b. (1994) *Teaching to Transgress. Education as the Practice of Freedom*. New York: Routledge.

hooks, b. (2003) *Teaching Community: A Pedagogy of Hope*. New York: Routledge.

Hutchinson, J., Bonetti, S., Crenna-Jennings, W. & Akhal, A. (2019) *Education in England: Annual Report 2019*. London: Education Policy Institute.

Ipsos, Mori (2020) State of the Nation: Understanding the Attitudes of the Public to the Early Years. Accessed 09.07.2021: https://www.ipsos.com/sites/default/files/ct/news/documents/2020-11/ipsos_mori_son_report_final.pdf

Jironet, K. (2020) *Feminine Leadership: Personal Development beyond Polarities*. 2nd Edition. London: Routledge.

Kaska, M. (2015) *Social Pedagogy – An Invitation*. London: Jacaranda Development.

Krieg, S., Davis, K. & Smith, K. A. (2014) Exploring the Dance of Early Childhood Educational Leadership. *Australasian Journal of Early Childhood*, 39(1), 73–80.

Leadbeater, C. (2020) Love Meets Power. The Australian Centre for Social Innovation. Accessed 13.07.2021: https://tacsi.org.au/wp-content/uploads/2020/06/TACSI_LovePower_Report.pdf

Legatum Institute (2020) UK Prosperity 2020 Report. Accessed 13.07.2021: https://li.com/reports/uk-prosperity-2020/

Lewis, M.W. (2000) Exploring Paradox: A More Comprehensive Guide. *Academy of Management Review*, 25(4), 760–76.

Louv, R. (2012) *The Nature Principle*. Chapel Hill, NC: Alqonquin Books.

Madsen, B. (2005) *Socialpædagogik [Social Pedagogy]*. Copenhagen, Denmark: Hans Reitzels Forlag.

Malaguzzi, L. (1993) For an Education Based on Relationships. *Young Children*, 49(1), 9–12.

Meyerson, D. E. (2008) *Rocking the Boat: How to Effect Change without Making Trouble.* Hoboken, NJ: Harvard Business Press.

National Audit Office (2020) Supporting Disadvantaged Families through Free Early Education and Childcare Entitlements in England. Accessed 13.07.2021: https:// www.nao.org.uk/report/supporting-disadvantaged-families-through-free-early-education-and-childcare-entitlements-in-england/

National Day Nurseries Association (2019) Annual Workforce Survey. Accessed 13.07.2021: https://www.ndna.org.uk/NDNA/News/Reports_and_surveys/ Workforce_survey/nursery_workforce_survey_2019.aspx

Nicholson, J. & Maniates, H. (2016) Recognizing Postmodern Intersectional Identities in Leadership for Early Childhood. *Early Years*, 36(1), 66–80.

Nicholson, J., Kuhl, K., Maniates, H., Lin, B. & Bonetti, S. (2020) A Review of the Literature on Leadership in Early Childhood: Examining Epistemological Foundations and Considerations of Social Justice. *Early Child Development and Care*, 190(2), 91–122.

O'Sullivan, J. (2015) *Successful Leadership in the Early Years.* London: Bloomsbury.

OECD (2018) Building a High-Quality Early Childhood Education and Care Workforce. Further Results from the Starting Strong Survey 2018. Accessed 13.07.2021: https://www.oecd-ilibrary.org/education/building-a-high-quality-early-childhood-education-and-care-workforce_b90bba3d-en

OECD (2019) Education at a Glance. Accessed 13.07.2021: https://www.oecd-ilibrary. org/education/education-at-a-glance-2019_f8d7880d-en

Ofsted (2011) Annual Report 2010-2011. Accessed 25.11.2021: https://www.gov.uk/ government/publications/the-annual-report-of-her-majestys-chief-inspector-of-education-childrens-services-and-skills-201011

Oliveira-Formosinho, J. & De Sousa, J. (2019) Developing Pedagogic Documentation: Children and Educators Learning the Narrative Mode. In Formosinho, J. & Peeters, J. (Eds.) *Understanding Pedagogic Documentation in Early Childhood Education* (pp. 32–51). London: Routledge.

Osinga, F.P.B. (2007) *Science, Strategy and War: The Strategic Theory of John Boyd.* Abingdon: Routledge.

Pascal, C. & Bertram, T. (2012) Praxis, Ethics and Power: Praxeology as a Participatory Paradigm for Early Childhood Research. *European Early Childhood Education Research Journal*, 20(4), 477–93.

Petrie, P. (2020) Taking Social Pedagogy forward: Its Fit with Official UK Statements on Promoting Wellbeing. *International Journal of Social Pedagogy*, 9(1), 17. DOI: https://doi.org/10.14324/111.444.ijsp.2020.v9.x.017

Philips, A & Taylor, B (2009) *On Kindness.* London: Penguin Books.

Prasad, R. (2008) *A Conceptual – Analytical Study of Classical India and Philosophy of Morals.* New Delhi: Concept Publications.

Putnam, R.D. (2000) *Better Together*. Simon & Schuster.

Reich, R. (2018) *The Common Good*. New York, NY: Knopf, Borzoi Books.

Rinaldi, C. (2006) *In Dialogue with Reggio Emilia: Listening, Researching and Learning*. Hove, UK: Psychology Press.

Robinson Hickman, G. & Sorenson, G. J. (2013) *The Power of Invisible Leadership: How a Compelling Common Purpose Inspires Exceptional Leadership*. New York, NY: Sage.

Rodd, J. (1996) *Leadership in Early Childhood*. Milton Keynes: Open University Press.

Rogers, M. (2005) Social Sustainability and the Art of Engagement—the Small Towns: Big Picture Experience. *Local Environment*, 10(2), 109–24.

Rogers, S., Brown, C. & Poblete, X. (2017) A Systematic Review of the Evidence-base for Professional Learning in Early Years Education (the PLEYE Review). Accessed 13.07.2021: https://discovery.ucl.ac.uk/id/eprint/10053553/1/Rogers_PLEYE_A%20 SYSTEMATIC%20REVIEW%20OF%20THE%20EVIDENCE_Nuffield.pdf

Sakr, M. & O'Sullivan, J. (Eds.) (2021) *Pedagogical Leadership in Early Childhood Education Conversations from across the World*. London: Bloomsbury.

Santone, S. (2019) *Reframing the Curriculum Design for Social Justice and Sustainability*. London: Routledge.

Schank, R. C. (1999) *Dynamic Memory Revisited*. Cambridge: Cambridge University Press.

Schein, E. H. (2016) *Organisational Culture and Leadership*. 5th Edition. Hoboken, NJ: Wiley.

Schein, E. H. & Schein, P. A. (2018) *Humble Leadership: The Power of Relationships, Openness and Trust*. Oakland, CA: Berrett-Koehler Publishers.

Schein, E. H. & Schein, P. A. (2019) *Humble Leadership: The Power of Relationships, Openness and Trust*. Oakland, CA: Berrett-Koehler Publishers.

Scott, K. (2017) *Radical Candour: How to Get What You Want by Saying What You Mean*. London, UK: Pan Macmillan.

Seldon, A. (2009) *Trust: How We Lost It and How to Get It Back*. London: Biteback Publishing.

Simpson, D., Mazzocco, P., Loughran, S., Lumsden, E., Clark, R. M. & Winterbottom, C. (2019) Parent–Practitioner Engagement in Early Education and the Threat of Negative Thinking about the Poor across England and the USA. *Research in Education*, 109(1), 20–36.

Smallbone, D., Evans, M., Ekanem, I. & Butters, S. (2001) *Researching Social Enterprise: Final Report to the Small Business Service*. London: Middlesex University.

Smith, W.K. & Lewis, M.W. (2011) Towards a Theory of Paradox: A Dynamic Equilibrium Model of Organising. *Academy of Management Review*, 36(2), 381–403.

Social Metrics Commission (2020) Measuring Poverty 2020. Accessed 14.07.2021: https://socialmetricscommission.org.uk/measuring-poverty-2020/

Stephen, C. (2010) Pedagogy: The Silent Partner in Early Years Learning. *Early Years*, 30(1), 15–28.

Stephens, L. & Hall, M. (2020) *Quality Childcare for All*. London: New Economics Foundation. Accessed 13.07.2021: https://neweconomics.org/2020/01/quality-childcare-for-all

Stephens, P. (2013) *Heart and Head*. Bremen: EHV.

Stodd, J. (2014) *The Social Leadership Handbook*. London: Sea Salt Learning.

Stodd, J. (2016) *The Social Leadership Handbook*. 2nd Edition. London: Sea Salt Learning Press.

Storr, W. (2019) *The Science of Storytelling: Why Stories Make Us Human and How to Tell Them Better*. New York: Adams Press.

Strehmel, P. (2016) Leadership in Early Childhood Education – Theoretical and Empirical Approaches. *Journal of Early Childhood Education Research*, 5(2), 344–55.

Stringer, E. T. (1999) *Action Research Second Edition*. Thousand Oaks, CA: Sage.

Sutton Trust (2021) Covid-19 Report. Accessed 14. 07.2021: https://www.suttontrust.com/our-research/coronavirus-impacts-early-years/

Syed, M. (2019) *Rebel Ideas: The Power of Diverse Thinking*. London: John Murray Publishers.

Tasgal, A. (2015) *The Storytelling Book*. London: LID Publishing.

The Trussell Trust (2021) End of Year Stats. Accessed 14. 07.2021: https://www.trusselltrust.org/news-and-blog/latest-stats/end-year-stats/

ThemPra (2015) The 3 Ps: The Professional, Personal and Private Self of the Social Pedagogue. Accessed 25.11.2021: http://www.thempra.org.uk/social-pedagogy/key-concepts-in-social-pedagogy/the-3-ps/

ThemPra (2018) The Professional, Personal, and Private Self of the Social Pedagogue. http://www.thempra.org.uk/social-pedagogy/key-concepts-in-social-pedagogy/the-3-ps/.

ThemPra (2021) The Professional, Personal, and Private Self of the Social Pedagogue. Accessed 13. 07.2021: http://www.thempra.org.uk/social-pedagogy/key-concepts-in-social-pedagogy/the-3-ps/

Úcar, X. (2012) Social Pedagogy in Latin America and Europe: Looking for New Answers to Old Questions. In J. Kornbeck & N. Rosendal Jensen (Eds.) *Social Pedagogy for The Entire Lifespan (Volume 1)*. (pp. 166–201). Bremen, Germany: Europäischer Hochschulverlag.

UNESCO (2014) Shaping the Future We Want. Accessed 14.07.2021: https://sustainabledevelopment.un.org/content/documents/1682Shaping%20the%20future%20we%20want.pdf

Venkataraman, B. (2009) Education for Sustainable Development. *Environment: Science and Policy for Sustainable Development*, 51(2), 8–10.

Weick, K.E. (1995) *Sensemaking in Organizations*. London: Sage.

Whalen, S. et al. (2016) A Development Evaluation Study of a Professional Development Initiative to Strengthen Organizational Conditions in Early Education Settings. *Journal of Applied Research on Children: Informing Policy for Children at*

Risk, 7(2), https://digitalcommons.library.tmc.edu/childrenatrisk/vol7/iss2/9/?utm_source=digitalcommons.library.tmc.edu%2Fchildrenatrisk%2Fvol7%2Fiss2%2F9&utm_medium=PDF&utm_campaign=PDFCoverPages

Winman, T. (2020) The Role of Social Pedagogy in a Digitalized Society. *The Educational Review*, USA, 4(3), 81–92.

Woodhead, M. (2006) Changing Perspectives on Early Childhood: Theory, Research and Policy. *International Journal of Equity and Innovation in Early Childhood*, 4(2), 1–43.

Woodrow, C. & Busch, G. (2008) Repositioning Early Childhood Leadership as Action and Activism. *European Early Childhood Education Research Journal*, 16(1), 83–93.

Yunus, M. (2007) Creating a World without Poverty. *Social Business and the Future of Capitalism*. New York: Public Affairs.

Zeng, S., Douglass, A., Lee, Y. & DelVecchio, B. (2021) Preliminary Efficacy and Feasibility of a Business Leadership Training Program for Small Child Care Providers. *Early Childhood Education Journal*, 49(1), 27–36.

Index